Model-Based Computer Vision

Computer Science:
Artificial Intelligence, No. 14

Harold S. Stone, Series Editor

Professor of Electrical and Computer Engineering
University of Massachusetts, Amherst

Other Titles in This Series

Model-Based Computer Vision

by
Rodney Allen Brooks

UMI RESEARCH PRESS
Ann Arbor, Michigan

$\begin{array}{l} TA \\ 1632 \\ .B76 \\ 1984 \end{array}$

18559577

9-17-82 Ac

Produced and distributed by
UMI Research Press
an imprint of
University Microfilms Inc.
Ann Arbor, Michigan 48106

Library of Congress Cataloging in Publication Data

Brooks, Rodney Allen.
Model-based computer vision.

(Computer science. Artificial intelligence ; no. 14)
"A Revision of the author's thesis, Stanford University,
1981"–T.p. verso.
Bibliography: p.
Includes index.
1. Image processing. 2. Computer graphics. I. Title.
II. Series.

TA1632.B76 1984   620.'00425'0285443   84-2416
ISBN 0-8357-1526-4

Contents

List of Figures

Acknowledgments

When I first came to Stanford, computer vision was the area of artificial intelligence that held least interest for me. As an incoming student, I was assigned Tom Binford as an advisor. He asked me to build a vision system. The ACRONYM system and this study are the results. I now think that vision and spatial reasoning are the critical areas of artificial intelligence. It is Tom who persuaded me of this. He has given gentle guidance and taught me much. He has been my strongest supporter in dealings with the outside world. This study itself has been improved greatly by Tom's many critical readings of earlier drafts. For all this I thank him sincerely.

Hans Moravec showed me by example the importance of optimism and perseverance. He has always been generous to the extreme with time and ideas, ready to loose a barrage of intellectual energy at the slightest provocation. It has been a rare privilege to have worked with him.

Apart from providing MACLISP system support over the years, Dick Gabriel has been a true friend. Barry Soroka has been the major user of the ACRONYM system. He has offered both extensive constructive criticisms and generous friendship.

There have been many people who have actively contributed to the ACRONYM system. Russell Greiner was my original partner. Although none of his code remains today, many of his early criticisms and suggestions have had strong influences on various parts of the system. David Lowe and Mike Lowry have contributed strongly to my work, both with code and ideas. A number of masters students have had fruitful shorter term affiliations with the project. They include Harold Westphal, Amy Plikerd, Michael Overmeyer, and Peter Oppenheimer. Harald, especially, made many useful suggestions concerning the modeling system.

Marty Frost and Rob Poor were aways more than willing to help me out when problems arose with system software or hardware.

There have been many other people at the Stanford Artificial Intelligence Lab who made it such a friendly and great place to work. At the risk of forgetting some, they include Harlyn Baker, Jim Bennett, Peter Blicher, Jim

Davidson, Mike Farmwald, Erik Gilbert, Ron Goldman, Norm Haas, Frank Liang, Juan Ludlow, Allan Miller, Shahid Mujtaba, Ken Salisbury, Steve Westfold, and Polle Zelleweger.

While at Stanford I received financial support from the Defense Advanced Research Projects Agency under contract MDA903-80-C-0102, from the National Science Foundation under contract DAR78-15914, and from an Alcoa Corporation grant.

Moral support has been provided from afar by Nui.

1

Introduction

An implemented and operational model-based vision system is described. Examples are given of its interpretation of images, including extraction of three-dimensional parameters from monocular images. Advances are presented in representation for geometric modeling of objects and objects classes, in techniques for manipulating nonlinear symbolic algebraic constraints, in geometric reasoning in incompletely specified situations, and in constructing algebraic constraints from image measurements. Both generic object classes and specific objects are represented by volume models which are independent of viewpoint. Complex real world object classes are modeled. Variations in size, structure, and spatial relations within object classes can be modeled. New spatial reasoning techniques are described that are useful both for prediction within a vision system, and for planning within a manipulation system. New approaches to prediction and interpretation are introduced, based on the propagation of symbolic constraints. Predictions are two-pronged. First, prediction graphs provide a coarse filter for hypothesizing matches of objects to image features. Second, prediction graphs contain instructions on how to use measurements of image features to deduce three-dimensional information about tentative object interpretations. Interpretation proceeds by merging local hypothesized matches, subject to consistent derived implications about the size, structure, and spatial configuration of the hypothesized objects. Prediction, description, and interpretation proceed concurrently, from coarse object subpart and class interpretations of images to fine distinctions among object subclasses, and more precise three-dimensional quantification of objects.

1.1 Model-Based Vision

Much recent artificial intelligence work in computer vision has been concentrated on extracting maximal information from an image using no a priori knowledge of the particular objects being viewed. Some techniques are based on physical considerations concerning the image producing process. Others have been suggested by physiological and psychological evidence.

Typically surfaces are identified and local properties such as their orientation are extracted. There is still a general problem of how to map from such local descriptions to a structural understanding of an image. It has not been seriously tackled during recent years. This study deals with that problem.

A program can be reasonably described as "understanding" an image only if it can relate image features to a representation of the world that exists independently of image features. This study describes an implemented system called ACRONYM. It is a domain-independent geometric model-based vision system. The user describes to ACRONYM classes of three-dimensional objects and their relationships in the world. The system tries to interpret images by identifying instances of modeled objects. At the same time it extracts three-dimensional information concerning the size, structure, and spatial location and orientation of the objects. The same models and reasoning processes can be used for other purposes, such as simulating and planning assembly tasks with manipulators.

Consider figure 1.1. It is stratified into a few different levels at which objects in the world could be represented. The levels are not all as distinct and as well ordered as the figure might imply, its spirit can be accepted for the purposes of discussion.

Figure 1.1.   Levels of representation—both model-based and image-
based.

Model		Image
Function	⇔	Function
⇓		⇑
Object	⇔	Object
⇓		⇑
Volume	⇔	Volume
⇓		⇑
Surface	⇔	Surface
⇓		⇑
Shape	⇔	Shape
⇓		⇑
Edge	⇔	Edge
⇓		⇑
Pixel	⇔	Pixel

At the top level is *function*. Often properties of objects can be deduced from functional or contextual descriptions. For instance knowing that something is a ground transport vehicle probably implies that it has wheels or tracks of some sort. Knowing that certain types of aircraft use an airport may allow us to deduce a minimum length of the runways. A chair could be described as something which is built for the purpose of being sat on by a human.

The physical structure of *objects* can be described in terms of their geometrical properties. These might include the *volumes* that they occupy, along with their spatial relationships to other objects in the world. Such descriptions need not be completely specific. Geometric classes of objects and spatial relationships can be described. While such descriptions of objects are not complete, they are adequate for a wide range of tasks.

Objects can be described locally in terms of their *surfaces*. This might be in the form of a local orientation of the surface and its direction relative to the camera.

The remaining levels of the diagram are all image description terms. *Shapes* describe regions in a monocular image. They are usually generated by parts of surfaces. Shapes and image *edges* are viewpoint dependent. Edges bound shapes. They can result from discontinuity in surface normal, self obscuration (where a surface is tangent to the line of sight), a discontinuity in the surface reflectivity, or a discontinuity in illumination.

The lowest level representation for an image is the *pixel* level. A digitized image is represented as a two-dimensional array of integers, each representing an intensity level sampled by the camera. The array is arranged so as to retain the geometry of the image plane of the camera.

Figure 1.1 is divided into two columns. The left side shows the progression working from models down to images, and the right shows a data-driven approach working from pixels up to high level descriptions of the world.

A useful vision system must somehow relate its a priori understanding of the world to the information in images given to it. Thus it must relate entities which appear in the top left of figure 1.1 to entities in the bottom right. There are many areas for research in making all the transitions between levels and across levels. Questions concerning what operations can or should be done at each level, and with what generality, need to be answered.

Much of the current work in computer vision is concentrating on the lower levels of the right side of the diagram. Barrow and Tenenbaum [7], Binford [12], Horn [32], Woodham [62], and others have based algorithms on considerations of the physics of the production of images. Others, principally David Marr's research group at MIT, (see Marr [39], Marr and Hildreth [40], and Grimson [27] for instance) have found in psycho-physical evidence suggestions for algorithms that might be implemented on conventional computers to extract information from images. Most of this work has not been concerned with making use of model-driven processing, nor with crossing over to the model side at higher levels. There have been a large number of fundamental scientific problems identified in the lower right areas of the diagrams which can be well posed independently of the types of processing and mappings which might go on in other parts of the diagram. This study is concerned with most of the rest of the diagram.

The approach taken in ACRONYM is to map from a priori object class descriptions to descriptions in terms of the same primitives as produced by the image description processes. This can be viewed as prediction of image features. Matching is done between image and object at that level. The matches are not conservative, and in the interest of not rejecting correct matches some incorrect matches may also be accepted. Then a mapping from image description terms to object model primitive terms is made, making use of both the information gained at the image description level match and the information included in the image description prediction. Incorrect matches are found to be inconsistent with the detailed models at this stage. Eventually a three-dimensional interpretation of the image is obtained in terms of the a priori models.

The ACRONYM system deals with mappings from geometric models down to edges, and from edges up to geometric descriptions. Most of the column cross-over information flow at the bottom of the diagram is from left to right. At higher levels it is bidirectional.

This approach to image understanding relies on four components: object models, prediction from models, interpretation of image descriptions in terms of models, and descriptions of images. This study deals with only the first three. The three components are tied together in ACRONYM by two threads. Geometric models and relationships are used to derive predictions and guide interpretation. Algebraic constraints are used to model class relationships, then to give a quantitative aspect to predictions, to prune incorrect interpretations, and to provide three-dimensional information about hypothesized objects.

ACRONYM does not make use of the rich image descriptions available from some of the recent work mentioned above. The descriptive work is still in active research stages, and robust program modules implementing the ideas are not available. Rather, it was decided to use a simple and primitive system which the author had previously built. ACRONYM currently uses the inaccurate and crude descriptions which that system produces. As better low-level descriptions are used, ACRONYM's performance must improve. Currently ACRONYM is forced to work downwards on the left further than may be strictly necessary, or useful, and transfers information across from model to image domains at lower levels (as well as higher levels) than recent work indicates will be necessary.

1.2 Contributions

This study makes contributions to a number of areas of research. They are linked by a central thesis:

> *For man-made objects, geometric classes of objects are meaningful and useful concepts. There are characterizations of observable features which are invariant over geometric classes of objects. It is possible both to identify instances of classes from observing those features, and, under the*

guidance of the invariant characterizations, it is possible to extract three-dimensional information from a monocular image by making measurements of the observed features.

The ACRONYM system, which is the implementation of many of the ideas in this study, is the first geometric modeling system that uses generalized cones with enough generality to be able to model real world objects in a nontrivial manner. Furthermore it is able to model geometric classes of objects, with algebraic constraints relating parameters of size, structure, and spatial relationships.

To handle such nonlinear algebraic constraints, a new set of methods have been developed for deciding satisfiability and for bounding expressions over satisfying sets.

Objects and their spatial relationships do not have all their parameters specified numerically in the representation developed above. Therefore techniques for geometric reasoning over incompletely specified situations were developed. In conjunction with the algebraic constraint manipulation system, these techniques are useful both for finding invariant characterizations of observable features, and in reasoning about change in a modeled situation, such as in planning manipulator tasks.

Finally, techniques for deriving algebraic constraints from noisy image measurements were developed. These rely on the identification of the invariant characterizations described above.

1.3 Outline of the Study

The following provides a guide to the contents of the study and plausible routes through it.

Chapter 2 is an overview of the ACRONYM system, describing its modules, their connections, and the flow of control. ACRONYM has been used by a number of other researchers for various purposes. The last section of chapter 2 describes briefly the uses they have made of the modules of ACRONYM described in this study.

Chapter 3 is a brief survey of other work in the fields of geometric modeling and model-based vision.

Chapters 4 through 8 constitute the five main contributions of the study. Each chapter surveys related work in the field, describes the computational problems involved, and explains the particular approach taken to solve these problems in the implementation of ACRONYM. Chapters 4, 5, and 6 can be read independently but 7 and 8 rely heavily on all three.

Chapter 4 deals with geometric modeling. Geometric modeling is often associated with modeling specific objects. Here the demands on geometric modeling are extended to include generic object classes, and partially specified spatial relationships between instances of object classes. A method to maintain complex internal relationships between parameters of object class instances is described.

The deductive power for implementations of the present paradigm for model-based vision is provided by a constraint manipulation system. Chapter 5 describes the formal requirements for the constraint manipulation system, and completely specifies the algorithms of the constraint manipulation system implemented for ACRONYM. It is demonstrated bounding nonlinear functions over nonlinearly defined subsets of real n dimensional space. The constraint system in conjunction with the geometric models of chapter 4 can be used in planning manipulator-based assembly tasks. The final section of chapter 5 gives an example of how the constraints can be used to check the validity of a planned assembly, and to provide guidance to decisions during the planning process.

An understanding of geometry is required to make full use of volumetric models and make inferences from their modeled spatial relations, no matter how incompletely specified. Chapter 6 describes methods for handling complex geometric relationships. It also provides methods for making deductions from the relationships between objects and the camera. Explicit rules are given which implement these methods.

Given geometric models ACRONYM tries to identify invariants and so set up expectations which direct low level descriptive processes and the actual interpretation of an image as instances of modeled objects. Chapter 7 describes how to make use of the geometric reasoning system and the constraint manipulation system to make invariant predictions concerning image features and their relations. Advance planning for how to make use of noisy image measurements to make three-dimensional deductions is also described.

Predictions provide local feature expectations along with expectations of relations between them. The interpretation algorithms described in chapter 8 try to find consistent matches for these expectations, resulting in labelings of image features, that possibly include some excessive labels. The algorithms therefore use the constraint manipulation system to detect algebraically inconsistent groupings, and to deduce, concurrently, three-dimensional information about the viewed objects.

Chapter 9 shows the ACRONYM system carrying out vision tasks in the domain of aerial photograph interpretation. Despite having little knowledge of the scale of the images, and very poor performance from low-level descriptive processes, ACRONYM successfully locates and identifies the type of aircraft in images of airfield scenes.

The final chapter expounds the contributions to spatial reasoning and computer vision that are made by this study. Principally these are concerned with representing and reasoning about incompletely specified geometric situations and identifying invariants over those uncertainties.

Appendix A1 gives the complete input specifications for some models used throughout the body of the study: generic wide-bodied passenger jet aircraft, generic small electric motors, and models for a screw insertion task discussed in chapter 5.

The second appendix (A2) describes the particular image description processes used in the examples of chapter 9. These consist of an edge finder written by Nevatia and Babu [46], and a ribbon and ellipse finder written by the author [20].

The modules described in chapters 6 through 8 are implemented either partly or wholly in terms of production rules. Appendix A3 gives a brief description of the rule compiler and some example rules.

2

The ACRONYM System

Figure 2.1 shows those modules and major conceptual data structures of
ACRONYM which are concerned with model-based vision. All except the edge
finder were designed and implemented by the author. It is a separate module
and runs as a preprocessor on grey level images (see app. A2 for a brief
overview).

The boxes labeled "data" are major data structures. The others are
logically separate program modules. The arrows indicate directions of
information flow.

ACRONYM is implemented in MACLISP and runs in two 256K word core
images on a DEC KL-10 under the WAITS operating system at the Stanford
Artificial Intelligence Laboratory. (A conversion package is under
construction which allows unchanged ACRONYM source files to run in FRANZ
LISP under UNIX on a VAX.) One core image contains the edge mapping
module and the other contains all other modules. (The core images
communicate with each other via files using a general purpose message
broadcasting system. More core images can be added without modifying the
first two; interlock avoidance is inherited from the WAITS file interlock
handling system.)

2.1 Model-Based Vision

This section describes how the modules of ACRONYM shown in figure 2.1 fit
into the model-based vision paradigm of four components: models,
prediction, description, and interpretation.

2.1.1 Models and Modeling

The user gives ACRONYM models of objects and their spatial relationships, as
well as classes of models and their subclass relationships. The first provides a
geometric component of the representation scheme, and the second an
algebraic component. Objects are modeled by the volumes they occupy and by
transforms between the local coordinate systems of those volumes. Classes

Figure 2.1. The Acronym system.

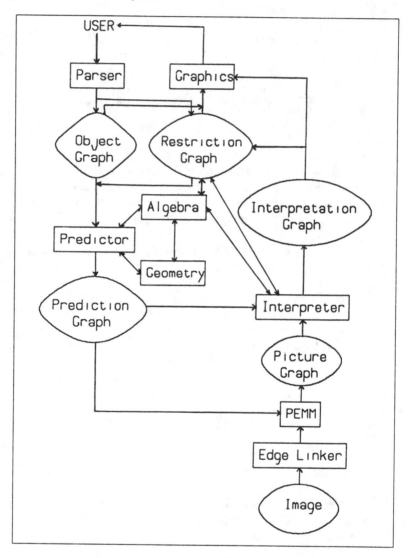

(and so subclasses) are defined by sets of inequalities (constraints) on algebraic expressions (perhaps nonlinear) over parameters of the geometric models.

There is a choice of input modes.

A text-based description language has proved to be more useful for describing classes of objects and their spatial relations. It can also be used to input geometric descriptions. Appendix A1 gives the complete text for modeling two generic model classes using this input module. It is often referred to as the "parser."

MODITOR (a MODel edITOR) implemented originally by Harald Westphal and Amy Plikerd, and revised and significantly expanded by Soroka [55], provides a GEOMED-like (see Baumgart [9]) interactive interface, via keyboard and graphics display. This tends to be more convenient for modeling specific geometric objects. The two input systems produce the same internal representation.

As algebraic constraints are input, they are simplified and checked for mutual consistency. Thus the modeling system must communicate with the constraint manipulation system.

Algebraic constraints make it possible to represent geometric variations in size, structure, and spatial relations. They provide a mechanism for representing limited forms of context information. Thus ACRONYM uses representation levels near the top of the strata given in figure 1.1.

Volumetric models and spatial relations are represented in the *object graph*. Volume elements form the nodes, while spatial relations and subpart relations form the arcs. Object class relations are represented in the *restriction graph*. Nodes are sets of constraints on volumetric models. Directed arcs represent subclass inclusion.

A graphics module provides feedback to the user during the modeling process via a raster display. It generates images of objects being modeled under the modeled camera conditions. The diagrams in this book were made by the graphics module. Figure 2.2 is an example of an ACRONYM model displayed by the graphics module.

ACRONYM does not yet incorporate model acquisition from images. Techniques of segmentation and description were developed by Nevatia and Binford [47] to build tree structured generalized cone models of objects detected using a laser range finder. Winston [61] has shown how to infer object classes over variations in both size and structure from examples and nonexamples of objects. Together these techniques seem to provide a strong basis for future work on teaching object class descriptions to ACRONYM by showing it examples whose component parts it would first instantiate to specializations of a library of qualitatively different generalized cone models, including both single cones and joined cones.

2.1.2 Prediction and Predicting

Geometric reasoning techniques are used to predict features which will be invariantly observable; i.e., features which will be observable over the modeled range of variations in size, structure, and spatial relations. Image relations between those features are also predicted.

Figure 2.2.   An ACRONYM model of a piston and crankshaft assembly.

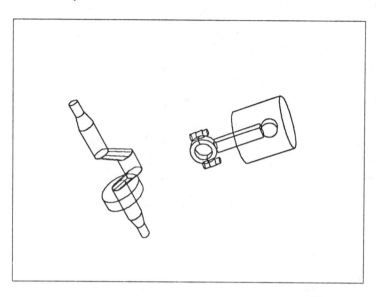

This requires analysis of the ranges of those variations in the object model classes. Notice that ACRONYM does not predict the complete appearance of objects from all possible viewpoints, but rather it predicts features which will enable it to identify instances of objects and determine their orientation and position. Sometimes case analysis is necessary to subdivide ranges of variations in order to establish observable features. The geometric reasoning module and the constraint manipulation system are heavily used.

One result of prediction is a set of instructions for low-level descriptive processes (see sec. 3.1.4). In the current ACRONYM implementation this corresponds to information transfer from left to right in figure 1.1 at the shape and edge level.

The other result of prediction is the *prediction graph*. The nodes of the graph are predictions of image features, and the arcs specify relations which must hold between them in the image. Predictions are two pronged. First, they provide a coarse filter for hypothesizing object to image feature matches; this is information transfer from left to right in figure 1.1 at the shape level. Second, they contain instructions on how to use measurements of an image feature to deduce three-dimensional information about the object to which it has been hypothetically matched. This corresponds to information transfer from left to right on figure 1.1 at the object and context levels, and includes information necessary for interpretation to transfer information back the other way.

The predictor is implemented as a set of production rules. (App. A3 outlines the rule system and gives some example rules in the form they are fed to ACRONYM.)

2.1.3 Description and Describing

The current implementation of ACRONYM uses two rather crude description modules. They are the weakest part of the ACRONYM system and are not covered in the body of this study.

The first is completely independent of the rest of ACRONYM and is run as a separate preprocessing stage on images. It produces descriptions of images in terms of straightened edges. It was imported from Nevatia and Babu [46] at USC. See appendix A2 for more details. Figure 2.3 (left) shows a set of lines produced from a grey level aerial photograph. There are typically about 1,000 edge elements produced, ranging between approximately 3 and 100 pixels in length, in a 512 by 512 image.

Figure 2.3.   At left is the low-level input to ACRONYM. At right are the ribbon descriptions returned by the descriptive processes when directed by predictions to look for shapes generated by the fuselage and wings.

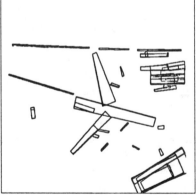

A module known as the PEMM (for Prototype Edge Mapping Module) takes the output of that module as one of its inputs. The other input to the module is one of the results of prediction (see sec. 2.1.2 above). Prediction provides goal-direction to an edge linking algorithm (Brooks [20]) which produces descriptions of shape elements found. Typically there are about 200 elements from a search of the whole image. Figure 2.3 (right) shows a set of ribbons (two-dimensional specializations of generalized cones) produced by the module under the direction of the predictor. Chapter 9 has more details of this and other examples. The descriptive process may be re-invoked many times during the interpretation of an image. At first the multiple invocations search for different image features to determine a coarse image interpretation. Later invocations search small areas of the image for particular features, both for detailed object class identification and to gain detailed three dimensional information about the objects.

There is a plan to later include other low-level descriptive processes, such as the stereo work underway within the Stanford vision group (Baker [6]).

2.1.4 Interpretation and Interpreting

Invocations of the descriptive processes provide candidate image features for matching to predicted features. Matching does not proceed by comparing image feature measurements with predictions for those measurements. Rather the measurements are used to put constraints on parameters of the three-dimensional models, of which the objects in the world are hypothesized to be instances. The constraint manipulation system is invoked to check for consistency. Only if the constraints are consistent with what is already known of the model in three dimensions are these local matches retained for later interpretation. A local match can thus constrain camera parameters, object size, and structure, or perhaps only relations between camera parameters and object size. Thus the interpretation module derives information about the particular instances of the modeled objects and their relationships.

This approach automatically handles, for instance, problems of scaling. Local matches are combined to form more global interpretations, but all constraints implied by local matches must be mutually consistent. Combining local matches may produce additional constraints which also must be consistent. Additional iterations of prediction, description, and interpretation occur as finer and finer details of objects are identified. Thus the interpretation module provides more precise information to the prediction module (via the models) enabling it to make meaningful predictions about finer details of objects.

Once a member of an object class has been identified, it is easy to check whether it is possible that the object is also a member of a subclass. It is merely a matter of checking whether the constraints introduced by the interpretation are consistent with constraints describing the subclass. The constraint manipulation system is invoked to carry out this computation.

2.2 Other Tasks

The ACRONYM system has been used by a number of other people for experiments in image understanding, and for a number of tasks other than image understanding. Their work is not, of course, a subject for this study, but

Figure 2.4.   An ACRONYM model of the hand-eye table
             configuration at the Stanford Artificial Intelligence
             Laboratory. This model is used for off-line
             programming using Soroka's SIMULATOR. The
             simulator detects collisons between the generalized
             cones in ACRONYM's *object graph*.

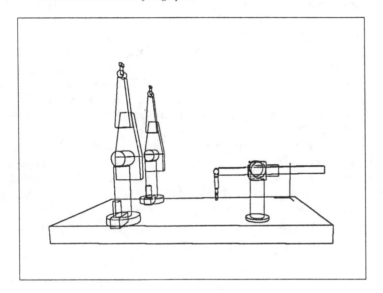

occasionally their requirements for ACRONYM have influenced design decisions made for the modules described in detail in later chapters.

D. Michael Overmeyer implemented a set of rules in an early version of the rule language used for the predictor and interpreter, useful for planning manipulator tasks. The system, GRASP (Binford [11]), was given ACRONYM models of simple objects from which it automatically deduced positions and orientations that could be grasped by a manipulator arm and that would provide a firm stable grip on the object. (Some of the problems encountered during that implementation helped convince this author to write a new rule system.)

Soroka [55] has built SIMULATOR on top of ACRONYM (see fig. 2.4). SIMULATOR is a system for off-line debugging of manipulator programs. It uses the ACRONYM modeling system to model manipulator arms and their environment. The graphics system is used to provide a stereo pair of images of the scenes so that the user perceives a three-dimensional model. Currently the system can be driven by the output of AL [26], which is normally used to drive manipulator arms directly. Instead SIMULATOR drives models of manipulators in real-time, by specializing the spatial relations between manipulator links. It detects collisions between objects without the disastrous consequences possible in the real world. SIMULATOR has also been used to design new hardware (a three fingered hand) and debug control systems for it, before fabrication.

Lowe [36] used line drawings produced by the graphics module, and coarse interpretations carried out by ACRONYM, as input to a system which numerically solved for absolute camera parameters (as distinct from symbolically solving for modeled camera parameters, which is what ACRONYM does).

Last, and least, the ACRONYM core image provides a convenient programming environment, adding many useful features to the underlying MACLISP. In addition to a wider range of control structures, graphics primitives, and translation of tail recursive functions into optimized iterative functions, there is a record package that provides structured data types and type checking. The record package compiles very efficient data referencing code (via a source to source translator and then the standard MACLISP compiler). It provides a wide range of procedural attachment capabilities (used extensively in ACRONYM to keep data structures self consistent). For these reasons the ACRONYM environment is routinely used for such diverse applications as research into edge detection algorithms, an electronic blackboard system, and for our research group's budget projections.

3

A Survey of Related Work

This study is about work in geometric modeling, spatial reasoning, and using models to direct vision. In this chapter we briefly survey related work in geometric modeling and model-based vision. More detailed surveys of geometric modeling, and from different perspectives to that offered here, can be found in Requicha [49] and Baer et al. [5].

3.1 Geometric Modeling

Geometric modeling systems are most commonly built as components of computer aided design systems (CAD). Less commonly, the primary intention is to build a geometric modeling system to drive a model-based vision system. Such is the case with ACRONYM's modeling system. Modeling systems built with either intention, however, share the problems of providing a representation which is convenient for the user, in the sense that the user must be able to readily decompose the objects to be modeled into the representational primitives.

Geometric modeling systems for CAD applications typically provide a small set of primitive volume elements which can be combined using set intersections and unions. Typical and well-known examples are the BUILD system of Braid [19], and the PADL system of Voelcker et al. [59]. Both use rectangular blocks, wedges, and cylinders as their primitives. There are certain restrictions on the directions of cylindrical axes relative to planar faces of other primitives. The BUILD system represents objects internally by keeping track of the edges produced by the intersections and unions. The PADL system retains a record of the set operations and the primitive volume elements used to build the object. Both systems are primarily intended to represent specific objects. The PADL system does allow the user to attach tolerances to parameters of the instances of the volume primitives. Both systems provide hidden line eliminated graphics output as their primary computations from the models. The PADL system also provides standard engineering-like drawings of the objects.

Baumgart [9] set out to build a geometric modeling system which would be used to drive a model-based vision system. He got side-tracked in the modeling stages and did very few vision experiments which made use of the system, called GEOMED, that he constructed. Rather than having volume primitives, Baumgart's system was engineered so that an experienced user could very quickly build general polyhedra. The user then added and subtracted such polyhedra to build more complex models. Again the intent was to build very specific geometric models. There was no notion of prototype at levels higher than simple polyhedra. The internal representation is based on the bounding edges of the planar polygonal faces of the polyhedra. The GEOMED system carries out full hidden line elimination and has mainly been used for producing drawings of modeled objects.

Grossman [29] built a procedural modeling system called GDP based on point primitives. They are combined procedurally into lines, and then lines are combined procedurally into polyhedra. Volumes are combined by set union and intersection. The system is designed only for modeling specific objects. By attaching extra procedures to the models at critical points, the modeling system can be used for different purposes. Wire frame drawings are thus simply produced. Grossman [28] investigated the propagation effects of tolerances by attaching statistics gathering procedures and running Monte-Carlo simulations over error distributions attached to the individual parameters. Lieberman [35] used a later version of GDP to predict the silhouettes that modeled objects could produce on a light table. These were used for recognition of objects in a model-driven vision system.

Miyamoto and Binford [44] built a modeling system based on generalized cones (see Binford [10]) arranged in a subpart, coarse to fine, hierarchical tree. The system carried out hidden line elimination and produced line drawings. Bolles [17] used these line drawings to predict features observable with Moravec's [45] *interest operator* (it detects local maxima of a directional variance measure) for a curve finder. Miyamoto's modeling system was used to model specific objects only, and Bolles system made predictions of observable features and their spatial relations in images for specific and completely determined orientations and positions of the objects relative to the camera. Again there is no notion of prototypes.

Agin [3] has recently developed a modeling system based on generalized cones arranged in a subpart tree. It is the modeling system closest to ACRONYM in capabilities. It can model objects of similar complexity to ACRONYM but is restricted to a much simpler class of generalized cones. In particular all of the surfaces are planar and cross sections are swept normal to straight spines. The system has a limited form of prototyping and some ability to specify relations between object parameters. Neither is as general as that provided by ACRONYM. Agin's system has no notion of geometric class. So far it has only been used for producing wire frame drawings.

3.2 Model-Based Vision

Previous model-based vision systems have generally not made a distinction between models of objects in world terms and models of objects in terms of directly observable image features. The models themselves have been descriptions of observable two-dimensional image features and relations among them. Some systems build the models themselves by being shown training examples. Others are given a priori models by the system user. This approach makes sense when it is desired that the vision system interface with an understanding of the world which is useful for other purposes. The following does not concern itself with systems whose only models are those built by themselves.

Barrow and Tenenbaum [7] with their MSYS system model objects as usually homogenous image regions. Garvey's [25] ISIS includes brightness, hue, and saturation of image regions in its object models which are constrained to meet viewpoint-dependent spatial relations. Ohta et al. [48] also model objects as image regions, but they include shape descriptions in two dimensions. Again viewpoint-dependent spatial relations are used.

Kanade [33] distinguishes the image domain, the domain of observable facts from viewing the scene in either intensity or range data, and the scene domain, where objects are modeled. He uses a two and a half-dimensional scene domain. Objects are represented as image regions. Shape and spatial relations describe the regions. Objects have multiple representations for multiple viewpoints, but these must be explicitly described by the user. The matching process tries to match observed patches against modeled patches.

The VISIONS system of Hanson and Riseman [30] is more ambitious, but again the models are essentially in image terms. Furthermore the low level descriptive processes run on a different machine to the higher level process, with magnetic tape as the interface medium. This implies a very loose coupling between the higher level knowledge and the low-level feature extraction.

Rubin's [50] ARGOS system stores multiple representations of buildings, in terms of such things as texture, color, orientation, and gross shape features, all gleaned from training examples. It also has user-defined three-dimensional knowledge of the positions of the buildings, which is translated into adjacency information to guide the search for labellings of pixels. The search technique is a very local pixel (or segment) based *"locus"* search. This localness means that adjacency is the only meaningful relation which can be used, so that most of the global three-dimensional knowledge is not really used.

For the general vision problem where exact contexts are unknown, and often even approximate orientations are unknown, with viewpoint-dependent image models there must be multiple models of a given object or object class. Instead, viewpoint-independent models should be given to the system. The resolution of the problem of multiple appearances from multiple viewpoints then becomes the responsibility of the vision system itself. For a model to be completely viewpoint-independent yet still provide shape information, it must embody the three-dimensional structure of the object being modeled. Volume descriptions are useful for other applications, too. Planning how to manipulate objects while avoiding collisions requires volume descriptions (e.g., [38], [55]). Objects can be recognized from range data given volume descriptions (e.g., [47] and [57]). For individual applications, additional information might be included—surface properties for image understanding, density of subparts for manipulation planning. Volume descriptions provide a common representational basis for various distinct but possibly interacting processes, each of which need models of the world.

Consider the situation where the vision system is one component of a much larger system that deals with models or representations of objects which will appear in the images to be examined. For example, in a highly automated production system we might wish to use the CAD model of some industrial part as the only description necessary for a vision system. It would be able to recognize, locate, and orient instances of the part when they later appear on a conveyor belt leading to a coordinated vision and manipulation assembly station, with no description further than the CAD model. It should not be necessary to have a human in the control path, whose task is to understand the CAD model and then to translate it in to a description of observable features for the vision system. CAD systems for industrial parts deal in models which are viewpoint independent and which embody a three-dimensional description of the volume occupied by the part (e.g., both the PADL system [59] and that of Braid [19] meet these requirements). The representation scheme should also facilitate automatic computation of observable features from models. Lieberman's system [35] provides for automatic computation of silhouettes of objects as they will appear in binary images. In general, more comprehensive descriptions of observable features provide for robust vision in situations which are not completely controlled.

4

Model Representation

The model representation scheme used in a vision system must be able to represent the classes of objects which the system is required to recognize. When the representation is in world terms rather than image terms, it is necessary that observables be computable from the representation.

The world is described to ACRONYM as volume elements and their spatial relationships, and as classes of objects and their subclass relationships.

ACRONYM's modeling system is based on generalized cones (Binford [10]) as volume primitives. In addition to this geometric representation there is an algebraic representational component that is used to describe classes.

A single simple mechanism is used within the geometric models to represent variations in size, structure, and spatial relationships. Sets of constraints on such variations specify classes of three-dimensional objects. Adding constraints specializes classes to subclasses and eventually to specific instances.

ACRONYM is by no means the first model-based vision system to use volumetric models. Baumgart [9] and Lieberman [35] both used polyhedral representations of objects. Nevatia and Binford [47] used generalized cones. However ACRONYM goes beyond these systems. It has the capability to represent generic classes of objects as well as individual specific objects, and situations which are only partially specified and constrained, as well as specific situations.

It is not claimed that ACRONYM's class mechanism is adequate for all image interpretation tasks. In fact some of the examples below may seem to have been carried out successfully in spite of the representation mechanism. Other vision and modeling systems however do not have even that capability.

The following description of the model representation centers around the types of things which must be represented about objects for a variety of image interpretation tasks. A volumetric representation for objects is described first. A method for describing variations in such models by describing allowed variations in place holders for object parameters is given. This method allows representation of variations in size, structure, and position and orientation of objects. A class mechanism, based on specializations of variations, is built orthogonally to the volumetric representations.

4.1 Volumetric Representation

Generalized cones have been used by many people both as the output language for descriptive processes working from range data (Agin [2], Nevatia and Binford [47], Soroka [54]) and for modeling systems for vision (Hollerbach [31], Marr [39], Marr and Nishihara [41], Miyamoto [44]).

Generalized cones (Binford [10]) provide a compact, viewpoint-independent representation of volume elements. A generalized cone is defined by a planar cross section, a space curve spine, and a sweeping rule. It represents the volume swept out by the cross section as it is translated along the spine, held at some constant angle to the spine, and transformed according to the sweeping rule. Each generalized cone has its own local coordinate system. A right-handed system is used such that the initial end of the spine is at the origin, the initial cross section lies in the y-z plane, and the x component of the directional tangent to the spine at the origin is positive. Thus for cones where the cross section is normal to a straight spine the latter lies in the positive x axis.

Figure 4.1 gives examples of generalized cones used as the primitive volume elements in ACRONYM's representation. They include straight and circular spines, circles, and simple polygons for cross sections and sweeping rules which can be constant, linear contractions or more generally, contractions linear in two orthogonal directions. Cross sections may be held at any constant angle to noncircular spines.

The internal representation of all ACRONYM data structures is frame-like in that each data object is an instance of a *unit*. Units have a set of associated *slots* whose *fillers* define their values (e.g., Bobrow and Winograd [16]). Figure 4.2 shows the unit representation of a generalized cone representing the body of a particular electric motor. Its cross section, spine, and sweeping rule units are also shown. It is a simple right circular cylinder of length 8.0 and radius 2.5 (the system currently does not enforce any particular units of measurement).

ACRONYM's volumetric representation is built around units of class *object* (a unit's class is given by its *class* slot; this corresponds roughly to the *self* slot of KRL units—see Bobrow and Winograd [16]). Objects are the nodes of the *object graph*. The arcs are units of class *subpart* and class *affixment*. Objects have slots for an optional *cone-descriptor* (which is filled with a pointer to a unit representing a generalized cone), *subparts* and *affixments* (which are filled with a list of pointers to instances of the appropriate class of units), and a few more that are not discussed here. Subpart and affixment arcs are directional, pointing from the object whose unit references them, to the object referenced in their *object slot*.

Figure 4.1.   A selection of generalized cones used by ACRONYM as
primitive volume elements.

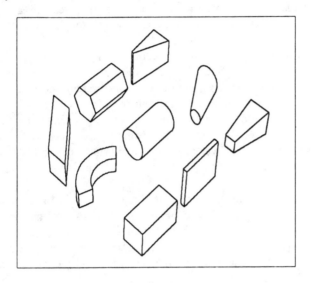

Figure 4.2.   A generalized cone model of a specific electric motor
body.

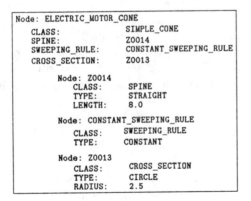

The object graph has two natural subgraphs defined by the two classes of
directional arcs. Connected components of the subpart subgraph are required
to be trees in this implementation. It is intended that each such tree be
arranged in a coarse to fine hierarchy. Cutting the tree off at different depths
gives models with different levels of detail. For example, the subpart tree for
the electric motors illustrated in figure 4.5 has a root-node whose cone
descriptor is the large cylindrical body of the motor. At the next lower level of

the tree are the smaller flanges and spindle. The coarse to fine representation has obvious utility in image understanding tasks. Unless ACRONYM has already hypothesized an interpretation of some image features as an instance of an object with its own generalized cone descriptor, it does not search for subparts of the object in the image.

Currently the user inputs the subpart trees directly; there is no enforcement of coarse to fine levels of representation. It is certainly within the capabilities of ACRONYM's geometric reasoning system (see chap. 6) to detect when the condition is violated. It is eminently reasonable that in such cases the system should build its own internal coarse to fine structure, while maintaining the user's hierarchical decomposition for future interaction. Resources have not been diverted to implement such a capability. There might be some problems with such a scheme in light of the discussion on *attachment* below.

Every object has its own local coordinate system. If an object has a cone descriptor, then the generalized cone shares the same coordinate system as the object. Affixment arcs relate coordinate systems of objects. An affixment includes a product of symbolic coordinate transforms, which transform the coordinate system of the object pointed at by the affixment to the coordinate system of the original object.

Coordinate transforms are represented as a pair (internally a unit with two slots) written *(r, v)* where r is a rotation and v is a translation vector. A rotation is represented as a pair (again a unit with two slots) written *(a, m)* representing a rotation of scalar magnitude m about unit axis vector a. A vector is a triple *(x, y, z)*. In this study, infix "*" will be used for composition both of rotations and of coordinate transforms, meaning that the left argument is applied following the right. Similarly, infix "$\otimes$" will be used for application of a left argument which is either a rotation or a coordinate transform to a vector as the right argument.

The affixments do not carry any connotation of attachment. For instance affixments do not distinguish between the case of the coordinate transform relating an electric motor sitting on a table, and the coordinate transform relating a permanently attached flange to the motor body. The attachment notion (whether rigid or articulated) is implied by the subpart relation. There are valid objections to such an assumption. A model of an operational airfield should include the fact that aircraft are usually present. The only way to represent such a fact in ACRONYM (see again the discussion of modality in sec. 2.2.3) is to make *aircraft* a subpart of *airfield*, and clearly in that case any assertion of permanent attachment is false. There may be some problems encountered from this aspect of the representation in planning manipulator tasks. There might also be problems in letting the system reorder the subpart tree to enforce a coarse to fine hierarchy as described above, as the reordering may destroy attachment relations intended by the user and introduce such relations which were not intended.

Both subpart and affixment arcs are represented by units. Subpart units have a *quantity* slot which specifies how many instances of a subpart an object has. For example the left-most electric motor in figure 4.5 has four identical flanges. The subpart relation for all four was represented as a single subpart arc between an electric motor and a flange node in the object graph. Affixment arcs similarly have a *quantity* slot. In the case of a quantity greater than one, the expression for the coordinate transform includes a free variable which is iterated over the specified range to produce the distinct coordinate transforms. That process produced the spatial relations of the numerous flanges to the electric motor bodies in figure 4.5.

Objects are placed in a world by affixing them to a world coordinate system. A camera position and orientation is described by affixing a camera unit to a world coordinate system. A camera views the world along the negative z-axis of its coordinate system, with the y-axis pointing in the direction of the top of the image plane, and the x-axis to the right. A *camera* unit also has a *focal-ratio* slot, which is filled with a number. The focal ratio r of a camera is defined so that the image of an object of length l which is parallel to the image plane of the camera, at distance d from along the line of sight, will measure rl/d in image plane coordinates. Figure 4.3 illustrates the coordinate system used.

Figure 4.3. The coordinate system used for ACRONYM camera models.

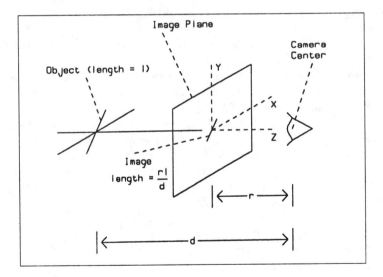

4.2 Quantification and Constraints

The previous section described how ACRONYM represents specific objects. On top of that representation scheme, a mechanism is built for representing classes of objects. The term *class* is used rather than *set* because a *criterial* or *intensional* augmentation of the volumetric representation is used. A class is the *extension* of a description of allowed variations in values of numeric slots of a volumetric model.

In KRL-type systems [16], it is usual to describe allowed variations of a slot filler by attaching a description directly to the slot. A different approach has been chosen for ACRONYM. Any numeric slot can be filled with an algebraic expression ranging over numeric constants, declared constant symbols, and free variables. The latter are referred to as *quantifiers*. The simplest case is when the expression is a simple numeric constant, which is exactly that described in the previous section. Declared constant symbols are purely for user convenience. Classes of objects are specified by supplying a set of *constraints* (inequalities on algebraic expressions) which define the set of values which can be taken by quantifiers. The benefits of such an approach are described below. Clearly this approach could be extended to allow variations in non-numeric slots, allowing for instance, that a quantifier range over a set of atomic symbols. The language of expressions for slot fillers and constraints would need to be extended to include non-numeric operators and comparators. Any such extensions would require a more comprehensive constraint manipulation system than the one described in chapter 5.

The PADL system [59] seems to be the only other geometric modeling system that allows detailed geometric models with quantifiable variations. Variations are limited to numeric tolerances on nominal values. The system uses a mixture of attaching descriptions of variations to slots and attaching them to named variables. Slots can be filled by expressions, but each term has a tolerance associated with it which propagates from the expression to the slot. A default tolerance is given to numbers and variables for which no explicit tolerance is given.

The current restriction of allowing variations in numeric valued slots of ACRONYM's representations still allows large generic classes of objects to be easily and naturally defined. For instance experiments with ACRONYM (see chap. 9) on aerial images have made extensive use of models of the generic classes of *airports* and *wide-bodied passenger jet aircraft*. Variations of numeric valued slots allows three distinct types of variations within a class of models; variations in size, limited variations in structure, and variations in spatial relationships. These correspond naturally to variations in the slots of generalized cones, in slots of the subpart tree, and in slots of the affixment tree respectively. Each of these is examined in more detail.

Figure 4.4.   A generalized cone model of a generic electric motor
body.

```
Node: GENERIC_ELECTRIC_MOTOR_CONE
    CLASS:              SIMPLE_CONE
    SPINE:              Z0014
    SWEEPING_RULE:      CONSTANT_SWEEPING_RULE
    CROSS_SECTION:      Z0013

        Node: Z0014
            CLASS:      SPINE
            TYPE:       STRAIGHT
            LENGTH:     MOTOR_LENGTH

        Node: CONSTANT_SWEEPING_RULE
            CLASS:      SWEEPING_RULE
            TYPE:       CONSTANT

        Node: Z0013
            CLASS:      CROSS_SECTION
            TYPE:       CIRCLE
            RADIUS:     MOTOR_RADIUS
```

4.2.1 Variations in Size

Figure 4.4 shows the unit representation of a generalized cone which is the body of a generic electric motor. Compare it to the cone for the specific electric motor of figure 4.2. The only difference is that the spine length and cross section radius slots are now filled with the quantifiers MOTOR_LENGTH and MOTOR_RADIUS respectively, rather than 8.0 and 2.5.

Consider the problem of representing a class of small electric motors that might be built on a particular assembly line. (Abraham et al. [1] describe a manufacturing situation where approximately 450 different styles of motors are manufactured with an average batch size of 600 and a number of style changes each day. The example models in this chapter [and app. A1] are loosely based on examples in that report. All dimensions are in inches.) Then the length and radius of the motor could be restricted independently, using the constraints:

$$6.0 \leq \text{MOTOR\_LENGTH} \leq 9.0$$
$$2.0 < \text{MOTOR\_RADIUS} \leq 3.0$$

Consider the problem of modeling motors of approximately the same weight and specifying the fact in the model. One approach is to put a constraint on an expression which is proportional to the motor volume, e.g.:

$$70.0 \leq \text{MOTOR\_LENGTH} \times \text{MOTOR\_RADIUS} \times \text{MOTOR\_RADIUS} \leq 160.0$$

To model motors of a particular volume or weight an equality could be used.

Notice that the last constraint relates the fillers of two distinct slots from two distinct units. Such a relation would be harder (or at least more clumsy) to specify if descriptions of allowed variations were attached directly to slots of units. In this case the description attached to at least one slot would have to explicitly refer to the other slot. If the system is to make use of new tighter constraints on either the length or radius to further constrain the other (this will be seen to happen during image interpretation in chap. 8) then the description attached to the two slots would have to refer to each other. If a relation exists between more than two slots, the situation becomes worse (such relations commonly arise during the image interpretation process). By placing the restrictions directly on quantifiers no such duplication of information is necessary.

Another benefit of attaching descriptions of allowed variations to quantifiers rather than to slots is that it becomes very easy to express many symmetries and other exact geometric relationships. For instance to specify that the wings of an aircraft are the same length it suffices to fill the length slots of the spines of the two wings with the same expression; e.g., just a single quantifier WING_LENGTH. Similarly to express the fact that a chair has four legs of the same length their spine length slots could all be filled with the quantifier LEG_LENGTH. Compare this to the representation of this fact used by Shapiro et al. [52].

The PADL system [59] allows the user to supply tolerances for object models, as described above. A different approach to tolerancing was used by Grossman [28]. He generates a large number of instances of models using a random number generator to produce varying dimensions of objects within prescribed bounds and distributions.

The ACRONYM system of constraining quantifiers allows tolerancing of objects in a simple manner. For instance suppose it was desired to represent a particular type of electric motor in figure 4.5 with length 8.0 ± 0.01 inches. Then simply the constraint

$$8.0 - 0.01 \leq MOTOR\_LENGTH \leq 8.0 + 0.01$$

could be used. Alternatively the spine length slot could be filled with the expression

$$8.0 + LENGTH\_ERROR$$

and the constraint

$$-0.01 \leq LENGTH\_ERROR \leq 0.01$$

used. Notice however that ACRONYM models need not be restricted to use only such simple plus-minus tolerances as are models in the PADL system. Tolerances can be specified using arbitrary algebraic expressions.

4.2.2 Variations in Structure

The fact that ACRONYM's subpart and affixment arcs are units with *quantity* slots allows a limited form of structural variation to be included in model classes. Filling the *quantity* slot of a subpart arc with 1 or 0 can be used to indicate the presence or absence of a subpart. The slot can alternately be filled with a quantifier constrained to be 1 or 0, to model the possibility that the subpart may or may not be present. Similarly a variable number of identical subparts of an object can be indicated; e.g., the number of flanges on the electric motors in figure 4.5, or the number of engines on an aircraft wing.

Figure 4.5.   Three specializations of the generic class of small
           electric motors.

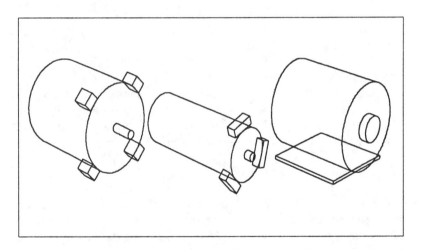

Figure 4.5 shows the generic model of an electric motor under three different sets of constraints which each fully determine values for the quantifiers BASE_QUANTITY and FLANGE_QUANTITY which fill the obvious *quantity* slots.

Given such a mechanism for representing structural variations, the question arises of what class of structure-varying models can be described. Consider the problem of specifying that an electric motor has either a *base* or *flanges* but not both. Furthermore if there are *flanges* then there are between 3 and 6 of them. This could be expressed with the following constraint:

((3 ≤ FLANGE_QUANTITY ≤ 6) < (0 = BASE_QUANTITY))
   < ((0 = FLANGE_QUANTITY) < (1 = BASE_QUANTITY))

Such a constraint is beyond the currently implemented capabilities of ACRONYM. Constraints must be algebraic inequalities, with an implicit conjunction over sets of such constraints. The explicit inclusion of logical disjunction requires a more comprehensive reasoning system for prediction and interpretation than the current system (see chap. 7 and 8).

Since the algebraic constraints can be nonlinear, it is possible to represent many things nonlinearly that would more naturally be represented as disjunctions. Furthermore this usually does not overtax the theorem prover. In fact the above constraint is equivalent to the following set of linear constraints:

$$0 \leq \qquad\qquad \text{BASE\_QUANTITY} \qquad\qquad \leq 1$$
$$0 \leq \qquad\qquad \text{FLANGE\_QUANTITY} \qquad\qquad \leq 6$$
$$\text{FLANGE\_QUANTITY} + 6 \times \text{BASE\_QUANTITY} \leq 6$$
$$3 \leq \text{FLANGE\_QUANTITY} + 3 \times \text{BASE\_QUANTITY}$$

However such a set of constraints is clearly not intuitive—unlike the previous constraint. The generic model of electric motors given in appendix A1 uses only the first two of these constraints.

In an ideal situation the modeling language should provide easy and natural means for the user to specify objects and classes in as much detail as is wished. The system should then sift out just enough detail of constraint for its own purposes. This problem is not tackled in this study.

4.2.3 Variations in Spatial Relationships

An affixment specifies the spatial relationship between two objects by providing a product of coordinate transforms which relate the local coordinate systems of the objects. Each coordinate transform consists of a rotation and a translation vector. The slots in the units representing these can naturally be filled with quantifiers or even expressions on quantifiers. Thus variable spatial relationships can be represented.

Suppose that members of the class of electric motors with bases are going to be placed at a work station, upright but with arbitrary orientation about the vertical, and at a constrained, but inexact position. The coordinate system of the motor has its x-axis running along the center of the spindle, and its z-axis vertical. The work station coordinates have a vertical z-axis also. The position and orientation of the motor relative to the workstation could then be represented by the transform:

$$((\hat{z},\ ORI),\ (X\_POS,\ Y\_POS,\ BASE\_THICKNESS + MOTOR\_RADIUS))$$

where $\hat{z}$ as usual denotes a unit vector in the z direction. Typically X_POS and Y_POS might be constrained by

$$0 \le X\_POS \le 24$$
$$18 \le Y\_POS \le 42$$

and ORI would be left free. The geometric reasoning system described in chapter 6 manipulates such underconstrained transforms.

There is an inadequacy in such specifications of spatial relations. It is possible to represent that aircraft can be found on runways or on taxiways, for instance, by affixing the generic model of an aircraft to both, using similar coordinate transforms to those described above. But, consider the case where it is desired to represent the situation for inspection in planning an assembly. Right after a pickup operation by a manipulator arm it may be desirable to use vision to check that it was successful. It would be convenient to be able to represent that the part which was to be picked up is now in exactly one of two positions; either its previous position in a feeder, say, or in the grasp of the manipulator hand. The only way within ACRONYM's representational mechanism to allow for such a possibility is to have it affixed to both places. This would direct the vision part of ACRONYM to expect an instance in both places. Again, the reasoning systems described in the rest of this study need major additions to handle a more concise specification language. Furthermore the current interpretation algorithm treats affixments as defining a necessary condition on where objects are located. A more flexible scheme would allow the user to give advice to look first in one location for a particular object, then in another higher cost location if that fails.

Variable affixments can also be used to model articulated objects. Figure 4.6 shows two views of a manipulator arm model with different values assigned to quantifiers filling the rotation magnitude slot of the joints. Constraints on the quantifiers express the range of travel of the joints.

The representation of articulated objects may be important if manipulator arms are present in images and it is desired to visually calibrate or servo them. Soroka's [55] simulator is based on these representations.

Variable camera geometry can also be represented by filling the slots of the transforms affixing the camera to world coordinates with quantifiers. Chapter 6 gives two examples of variable camera geometries. If the characteristics of the imaging camera are not known exactly, the *focal-ratio* slot can be filled with a quantifier rather than a number. Any image interpretation will provide information which can be used to constrain this quantifier (see chap. 8 for how this comes about).

Figure 4.6.   Variable affixments are used to model articulated
            objects such as this manipulator arm.

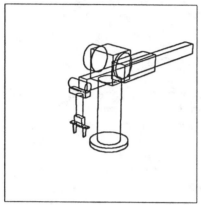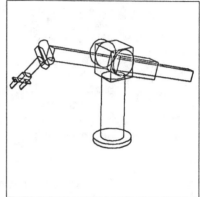

4.3 Restriction Nodes and Specialization

From the foregoing discussion it should be clear that given a volumetric model which includes quantifiers in various of its slots, different sets of constraints on those quantifiers define different classes of models. Sets of constraints are organized using units of class *restriction* as nodes in a directed graph called the *restriction graph*.

A *restriction* unit has a *constraint* slot filled by a set of algebraic constraints on quantifiers. The constraints used earlier in this section are typical examples, although they are reduced to a normal form described in section 5.4.1. A set of constraints on n quantifiers defines a subset of n-dimensional Euclidean space. It is the set of substitutions for the quantifiers which satisfy the given set of constraints. That set may be empty. This set is called the satisfying set of the restriction node. Set inclusion on the satisfying sets provides a natural partial order on restriction nodes, defining a distributive lattice on them. The lattice meet operation ($\wedge$) is used during image interpretation (see chap. 8). Arcs of the restriction graph must be directed from a less restrictive node (a larger satisfying set) to a more restrictive node (a smaller satisfying set). Restriction nodes keep track of the arc relations in which they participate via *suprema* and *infima* slots which are filled with lists of sources and destinations of incoming and outgoing arcs respectively. It is permissible that comparable restriction nodes do not have an explicit arc indicating that fact. In fact the restriction graph is just that part of the restriction lattice which has been computed.

A restriction graph always includes a *base-restriction* node, which has an empty set of constraints, and is thus the least restrictive node in the graph.

Every other node in the graph must be an explicitly indicated infimum of another restriction node.

The user specifies part of the restriction graph to the system. Other parts are added by ACRONYM while carrying out image understanding tasks. By contrast the object graph is completely specified by the user, perhaps from a CAD data-base, and remains static during image interpretation. Eventually ACRONYM may be able to build from examples, using techniques of Nevatia and Binford [47].

Restriction nodes have *type* and *specialization-of* slots. In nodes specified by the user, the *type* slot is filled with the atom *model-specialization* and the *specialization-of* slot with an object node from the object graph.

A restriction node specified by the user represents an object class: those objects which have the volumetric structure modeled by the object in the *specialization-of* slot subject to the constraints associated with the restriction node.

Thus the arcs of the subgraph defined by the user specify object class specialization. The arcs added later by ACRONYM also indicate specialization, but of a slightly different nature. They can specialize a model for case analysis during prediction (see chap. 7), or they can indicate specialization implied for a particular instance of the model by a hypothesized match with an image feature or features (see chap. 8).

Figure 4.7.   Part of the restriction graph: a model class hierarchy
                    defined by the user.

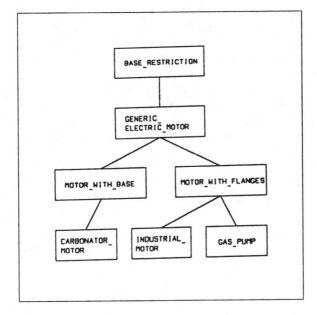

Figure 4.7 is a typical example of the portion of the restriction graph which the user might specify. The constraints associated with the node *generic-electric-motor* would be those described in the previous sections. The *motor-with-base* node includes the additional constraints:

$$BASE\_QUANTITY = 1$$
$$FLANGE\_QUANTITY = 0$$

while the *motor-with-flanges* node has:

$$BASE\_QUANTITY = 0$$
$$3 \leq FLANGE\_QUANTITY \leq 6$$

Of course additional constraints on quantifiers determining size, and perhaps their relationships to say, FLANGE_QUANTITY, which determines structure, might be included at these restriction nodes.

Additional constraints specialize the sub-classes of electric motors further to particular functional classes (these classes are taken from [1]), namely *industrial-motor, carbonator-motor,* and *gas-pump.* Further constraints on these three classes were added to restrict each quantifier to specific values in order to produce figure 4.5, which shows instances of the three classes of motor in left to right order.

The specialization mechanism described here relies on complete sharing of the volumetric description among all its specializations. There are never mulitiple copies of fragments of the volume model. The specialization information is in a domain orthogonal to the underlying representation. It is therefore compact. More importantly, during image interpretation, when an instance of a superclass has been identified it is rather easy to check whether it happens to also be an instance of a more specialized class. Instead of it being necessary to recompute image to model correspondence for the specialized model, it suffices to simply take the meet of the specialization restriction node with a restriction node produced in the original interpretation. If the resultant restriction node has a nonempty satisfying set then the perceived object is also an instance of the subclass. Chapter 8 describes this in more detail.

5

Constraint Manipulation

This study talks about a number of techniques that can be used in understanding what objects in a three-dimensional world produced a given image. These include volumetric representation of generic classes of three-dimensional objects, concise representation of generic spatial relationships, geometric reasoning about uncertain situations, generic prediction of appearance of objects, and use of information from matches of image features predicted and discovered by goal-directed search to gain three-dimensional knowledge of what is in the world. All these pieces are tied together by using systems of constraints (but there is no need to solve such systems!) In the current implementation of ACRONYM those constraints are algebraic inequalities over a set of variables (quantifiers).

This chapter describes some implementation-independent requirements for a "constraint manipulation system" (a CMS) in an ACRONYM-like system, and then the particular system which we have implemented and use. Finally some examples of its use on some robot manipulator planning subtasks are given.

5.1 Algebraic Constraints in Artificial Intelligence

Systems of algebraic constraints have arisen in a number of domains of artificial intelligence (AI) research.

Bobrow [15] used algebraic problems stated in English as a domain for an early natural language understanding system. The proof of understanding was to find a correct solution to the algebraic constraints implied by the English sentences. The domain was restricted to those sentences that could be represented as single linear equations and for which constraint problems could always be solved by simple linear algebra.

Fikes [24] developed a heuristic problem-solving program, where problems were described to the system in a nondeterministic programming language. The constraints were a mixture of algebraic relations and set inclusion statements over finite sets of integers. Fikes could thus solve constraint systems by backtracking, although he included a number of heuristic constraint propagation techniques to prune the search space.

A common source of algebraic constraint systems is in systems for computer aided design of electronic circuits. Stallman and Sussman [56] and de Kleer and Sussman [34] describe systems for analysis and synthesis of circuits respectively. In each case, systems of constraints are solved by using domain knowledge to order the examination of constraints and propagate maximal information from one to the next. An algebraic simplifier is able to reduce these guided constraints to simple sets of (perhaps nonlinear) constraints which can be solved by well-known numeric methods. The original constraints usually form too large a system to be solved in this way.

Borning [18] describes an interactive environment for building simulations of things such as electrical circuits, constrained plane geometrical objects, and simple civil engineering models. Algebraic constraints are used to specify the relations to be maintained in the simulation. Borning uses the constraint propagation technique described above, along with the dual method of propagating degrees of freedom among variables. When all else fails he uses a relaxation technique which first approximates the constraints with linear equations, then uses least-mean-squares fit to guide the relaxation.

There are two main requirements for ACRONYM's CMS. First, it must be able to decide (partially, see below) whether a set of constraints is satisfiable. This is a weaker requirement than asking that the CMS provide a solution for a set of constraints when one exists, such as is done by the previously described systems. It is not necessary to find an actual solution (there may be many), but rather whether it exists. Second, the CMS is used to estimate bounds on algebraic expressions on quantifiers over the satisfying set of values for the quantifiers. This is quite different from the tasks required of other CMSs.

5.2 Requirements for a CMS

Chapter 4 noted that a set of constraints on n quantifiers defines a subset of n-dimensional euclidean space corresponding to all possible sets of substitutions for the quantifiers such that all the constraints are simultaneously satisfied. Given a set S of constraints the satisfying set is written as C_S. In the following sets of constraints and restriction nodes are used interchangeably, as, in general, instances of each are associated with unique instances of the other.

The algorithms presented in the remainder of this study use the constraint manipulation system in three ways. In decreasing order of importance it would be ideal if the CMS could.

I1.   Given S decide whether or not C_S is empty.

I2.   Given satisfiable S and an expression E over quantifiers constrained by S compute the supremum and infimum of values achieved by E over the set of substitutions C_S.

I3.   Given constraint sets S and R calculate a constraint set T such that $C_T = C_S \cap C_R$; i.e. in the lattice defined in section 4.3, $T = S \wedge R$.

If the constraints were always linear in the quantifiers then it would not be hard to construct a CMS to behave as required, based on the simplex method. See section 5.4 for further details. (Clearly I3 can be simply achieved by letting $T = S \cup R$.)

However the algorithms to be described use the CMS as a pruning tool, in searches for invariant predictions, and for interpretations. Imperfect pruning does not necessarily lead to failure of the algorithms. It may lead to an increase in the portion of the search space which must be examined. If the pruning is very poor, the algorithms may fail to find predictions and interpretations for lack of storage space and time.

Now the above requirements are revised to those actually required by the prediction and interpretation algorithms, independent of the heuristic power which is required for efficient operation of those algorithms.

A1.   Given S, partially decide whether or not C_S is empty; i.e. if C_S is nonempty, return "don't know," and if C_S is empty return either "empty" or "don't know." Conversely this can be stated as *if the CMS can prove that S is unsatisfiable, it should indicate so, otherwise indicate that it may be satisfiable.*

A2.   Given satisfiable S and an expression E over quantifiers constrained by S, compute an upper bound on the supremum and a lower bound on the infimum of values achieved by E over the set of substitutions C_S; i.e. compute l and u (numbers, or $\pm\infty$) such that

$$l \leq \inf_{C_S} E \leq \sup_{C_S} E \leq u$$

A3.   Given constraint sets S and R calculate a constraint set T such that:

$$(C_S \cap C_R) \subseteq C_T \subseteq (C_S \cup C_R)$$

Note that for T derived from S and R as in A3, if C_T is empty then so is $C_S \cap C_R$ (which is equal to $C_{S \cup R}$). At first sight it may seem strange that a straightforward requirement such as I3 be relaxed to that of A3. First, since the prediction and interpretation algorithms can operate under A3, it is only a search efficiency consideration in deciding to settle for the weaker requirement. Second, it may be that the CMS works better on sets of constraints in some particular form. It may not be the case that if S and R have that form, then necessarily so will $T = S \cup R$.

While not strictly necessary it is also desirable that the CMS be monotonic, where monotonicity is defined as follows. If T is a constraint set derived from S and R as in A3, and in particular if $T \supseteq S$ then:

M1. If the CMS decides S is unsatisfiable then it also decides that T is unsatisfiable.

M2. For an expression E, if l_S and u_S are the bounds on E over S calculated as in A2, l_T and u_T the bounds over T similarly calculated, and both C_S and C_T are both nonempty, then:

$$l_S \le l_T \le u_T \le u_S$$

In section 5.4 the CMS implemented as part of ACRONYM is described. It is capable of meeting the above requirements for a wide class of nonlinear constraints. It is monotonic.

5.3 Algebraic Simplification

A brief digression follows to discuss some issues involved in algebraic simplification and the idea of reducing all algebraic expressions to a canonical symbolic form. Any algebraic constraint manipulation system needs a simplifier to make use of the results of formal manipulations of expressions.

De Kleer and Sussman [34] describe their experience with an algebraic simplification system which mapped all algebraically equivalent expressions into a canonical form as the ratio of two relatively prime multivariate polynomials. Each variable has a global priority used to determine the main variables of the polynomials and other orderings recursively. They point out that the canonical form is sometimes not compact, and the size can vary greatly if the variables are globally reordered. More importantly they discovered the algebraic manipulator spent most of its time and space calculating greatest common divisors (GCDS) of polynomials. When their circuit synthesis system failed due to lack of storage, it was always because of intermediate requirements of a single GCD calculation whose solution was actually quite small. They point out that their system is forced into doing much more complex manipulations than would ever be attempted by a human engineer.

The solution to this problem is to have a system that uses a simplifier which can handle more complex cases than a single canonical form. Furthermore, the system should be at least mildly intelligent in what it requests of the simplifier. Lastly, it would be advantageous if the higher level system were robust in the following sense. Suppose the simplifier returns a complex expression which is really equal to 0 (since there is no insistence on a canonical form, the simplifier may not have discovered this). Suppose further that the higher level system eventually has to abandon that expression because it is greater than some complexity bound. A robust system's outward behavior would not necessarily be affected by such failure, as it would possibly find some other approach to take. The algorithms to be described in chapters 7 and 9 for prediction and interpretation have some of this flavor.

5.3.1 ACRONYM's Algebraic Simplifier

ACRONYM's algebraic simplifier treats the symbols ∞ and $-\infty$ in the same way as numbers, and they are included below in references to numeric expressions. The simplifier propagates them through operators such as $+$, $\times$, max, min, etc., where such propagations are well defined.

The simplifier has special knowledge about how to handle $+$, $-$, $\times$, $/$, $\sqrt{}$, max and min (other functions such as sin and cos are treated purely syntactically, and no trigonometric identities are used). ACRONYM's CMS makes heavy use of expressions involving max and min. The expressions representable can not even be tested for equality syntactically. For instance the expression $A \max(B,C)$ is equal to $\max(AB,AC)$ if the expression A is positive, but equal to $\min(AB,AC)$ if A is negative. Thus a syntactic canonical form is not possible. There has been no attempt to develop a semantic canonical form, but instead there is increased interaction between the simplifier and the constraint manipulation system which uses it. Of course, inclusion of sin and cos makes the problem of simplification to a canonical form even more difficult.

The exact details of the standard form produced by the simplifier are not important. For the purpose of following the explanation of the constraint manipulation system given in section 5.4, it is sufficient to note that all instances of "$-$" are removed (multiplication by -1 is used where necessary), and quotients always have a numerator of 1. In general multiplication is distributed over addition, and addition is distributed over max and min as are multiplication and division, where possible.

The correctness of distributing division over max and min depends on the original arguments to those functions (unlike the multiplication case which depends only on properties of the term being distributed, as in the example above). For instance the simplification:

$$\frac{1}{\min(A,B)} = \max\left(\frac{1}{A}, \frac{1}{B}\right)$$

can not be made when A and B are of different signs. If their signs can not be determined in advance therefore, the simplification should not be made. When invoked by the CMS however ACRONYM's simplifier will not return an expression having the form of the left of the above equation; doing so can lead to nonmonotonicity of the system as described in point M2 of section 5.2. Instead it returns expressions which may not be equal to the supplied expression. For instance, given the expression on the left above, the simplifier is guaranteed to return an expression smaller or equal. Since such an expression can only arise as a lower bound on some quantity (see sec. 5.4.2) this "simplification" results in at worst a weaker bound. For instance given the expression:

$$\frac{1}{\min(A,B,C,D)}$$

the simplifier interacts with the CMS to try to determine the sign of the expressions A, B, C, and D using a method described in section 5.4.1. Suppose it determines that A and C are strictly negative, D is strictly positive, and the CMS can not determine the sign of expression B. Then the simplifier will return the possibly smaller expression:

$$\max(\frac{1}{A}, \frac{1}{C}).$$

If the original expression had been:

$$\frac{1}{\max(A,B,C,D)}$$

then given the same information about the signs of subexpressions, the simplifier would return the possibly larger expression:

$$\frac{1}{D.}$$

Since such an expression could only arise as an upper bound, the result is merely a weaker bound.

Finally, note that every term in a simplified expression is invariant when simplified by the simplifier.

5.4 A Particular CMS

The general requirements in section 5.2 stated for a CMS can be satisfied by the well-known linear programming simplex method in the case that all the constraints are linear. Finding whether a set of constraints is satisfiable is the first step of simplex—determining whether there is a feasible solution. Finding a bound on an expression is referred to as maximizing, or minimizing, a linear objective function. By the nature of the simplex method, it seems unlikely that it can be extended to nonlinear cases. An example of a nonlinear constraint arising in model definition was seen in section 4.2.1. Nonlinear constraints are also regularly generated in image interpretation as will be seen in chapters 7 and 8.

The CMS implemented for ACRONYM is based on another method which solves linear programming problems. This is the "SUP-INF" method, developed originally by Bledsoe [13], [14], and later improved by Shostak [53]. They developed it as part of a method for determining the validity of universally quantified logical formulas on linear integer expressions. These formulas often arise in program verification systems.

The linear method described by Shostak has been taken and extended it in a fairly natural way to handle certain nonlinear cases. A method of bounding difficult satisfying sets by n-space rectangloids, when straightforward extensions to the method fail or are not applicable, has been integrated into the original. This additional method was the major part of an earlier attempt by the author to build a CMS. By itself it weakly meets the requirements of the previous section and may be adequate for some interpretation tasks, where fine distinctions need not be drawn and where structural considerations (see chap. 7) remove most ambiguities.

5.4.1 A Normal Form for Constraints

Algebraic constraints are supplied to the CMS in a variety of forms. A set of given constraints are incorporated into a consistent normal form; an implicit conjunction over a set of inequalities using the relation "$\leq$" where at least one side is a single variable, and the other side consists of numbers, variables and the operators $+$, $/$ with numerator 1, $\times$, sin, and cos. Furthermore every such constraint derivable from the supplied constraint is merged into the constraint set. Much of the work is done directly by the algebraic simplifier.

Constraint sets are actually attached to restriction nodes in ACRONYM's implementation. Constraints in the normal form are grouped into subsets, determined by the variable which appears alone on one side of the inequality. Constraints with single variables on both sides appear twice, once in each "subset"—for example $a \leq b$ is associated both with variable a and variable b.

A new constraint is split into one or more inequalities. Constraints involving an equality are split into two inequalities: $A = B$ becomes $A \leq B$ and $A \geq B$. Thus, for instance, the constraint $x = y$ eventually becomes four inequalities; $y \leq x$ and $x \leq y$, which are associated with x, and $x \leq y$ and $y \leq x$, which are associated with y. A constraint such as $A \in [B, C]$, where A, B, and C, are expressions, can similarly be broken into two inequalities. The operators max and min are removed and equivalent constraints derived where possible (if not possible, then the constraint is discarded, and if externally generated the user is warned; there should never be such constraints generated internally). Thus, for instance, $\max(A, B) \leq \min(C, D)$ becomes the four constraints $A \leq C$, $A \leq D$, $B \leq C$ and $B \leq D$.

Next the constraints are "solved" for each variable which occurs in them; i.e. each variable is isolated on one side of the inequality. Since inequalities are involved, the signs of variables and expressions are important for these solutions. Sometimes the signs can not be determined, but often they can be deduced simply from explicit numeric bounds on variables given in earlier constraints (see the discussion of *parity* below). Finally inequalities using "$\geq$" are converted to use "$\leq$".

For example, given prior constraints of $y \leq -1$ and $x \geq 0$, the addition of constraint $x/y \leq \min(-100, 200 - z)$ generates the following set of constraints:

$$0 \leq x \qquad\qquad x \leq \infty$$
$$-100y \leq x$$
$$200y - yz \leq x$$
$$-\infty \leq y \qquad\qquad y \leq -1$$
$$-x/100 \leq y$$
$$\frac{1}{200/x - z/x} \leq y$$
$$-\infty \leq z \qquad\qquad z \leq \infty$$
$$\qquad\qquad\qquad z \leq 200 - x/y$$

Constraint sets generated by the CMS always contain single numeric upper and lower bounds on each variable—defaulted to ∞ or $-\infty$ if nothing more definite is known. If a new numeric bound is added for some variable, it is compared to the current bound (since they are both numeric or ∞, or $-\infty$ they are comparable), and the tighter bound is used.

Constraint sets are accessed by two pairs of functions. Given a set of constraints S, and a variable v, $HIVAL_S(v)$ and $LOVAL_S(v)$ return the numeric upper and lower bounds respectively that are represented explicitly in S. For instance given the example set E of constraints above, $HIVAL_E(x)$ returns ∞ and $LOVAL_E(x)$ returns 0. (The CMS using SUP defined below is able to determine that 100 is the largest value x can have and still satisfy all the constraints in E.)

More generally the constraint sets are accessed via the functions UPPER and LOWER which return the symbolic upper and lower bounds on a variable, represented explicitly in the constraint set. $UPPER_S(v)$ constructs an expression which applies min to the set of upper bounds on x appearing explicitly in S. The algebraic simplifier SIMP is applied and the simplified expression returned. Similarly $\text{LOWER}_S(v)$ returns the symbolic max of the explicit lower bounds. Thus, for instance, $\text{LOWER}_E(x)$ returns "max(0, $-100y$, $200y -yz$)," while $\text{UPPER}_E(z)$ constructs "min(∞, $200 - x/y$)" which gets simplified to "$200 - x/y$." These definitions of UPPER and LOWER closely follow those used by Bledsoe [13] and Shostak [53]. They did not use HIVAL and LOVAL.

A brief digression follows to explain an important use of HIVAL and LOVAL. They are used by the algebraic simplifier to try to determine whether an expression is always non-negative (this is loosely referred to as positive) or always negative. This information will be called the *parity* of an expression. If $\text{LOVAL}_S(v)$ and $\text{HIVAL}_S(v)$ have the same sign for a variable v, then v has a parity determined by the sign. If the lower and upper numeric bounds on v have different signs, then say that v has unknown parity. A few simple rules are used to try to determine the parity of more complex expressions. For instance the sum or product of two terms with the same known parity, shares that parity. The inverse of a term with known parity has that same parity. More complex rules are possible—they have not been used in ACRONYM.

Consider again the problem of producing a normal form for constraint sets. As symbolic bounds are added, an attempt is made to compare them to existing bounds. This is done by symbolically subtracting the new bound from each of the old, simplifying the resulting expressions, and applying the parity determining function. Whenever a parity for the difference can be found, the bounds are comparable over the ranges of variables given by HIVAL and LOVAL, and the stronger bound can be determined from that parity.

These techniques can be used to meet requirement A3 of section 5.2 In fact they also meet the ideal requirement I3, but they do more than merely form the union of constraint sets. Instead an equivalent set of constraints is produced which allows for efficient operation of the bounding algorithms described in the next section.

5.4.2 Bounding Algorithms

In this section algorithms are described which are used to estimate upper and lower bounds on expressions over satisfying sets of constraint sets. They satisfy the requirements of A2 of section 5.2. They are monotonic also. The partial decision procedure is based on these algorithms (see sec. 5.4.3).

The major algorithms SUP, SUPP, and SUPPP are described in figures 5.1, 5.2, and 5.3, respectively. There are three similarly defined algorithms INF, INFF, and INFFF whose definitions can be derived from the others by simple textual substitutions. The necessary substitutions for each algorithm are described in the captions of the appropriate figures.

Figure 5.1. Definition of algorithm SUP and lexical changes
needed to define algorithm INF.

IF	ACTION	RETURN
1. J is a number		J
2. J is a variable		
2.1 $J \in H$		J
2.2 $SUP_S(J, H)$ is already on the stack		$HIVAL_S(J)$
2.3 $J \notin H$	Let $A \leftarrow UPPER_S(J)$ $B \leftarrow SUP_S(A, H \bigcup \{J\})$	$SUPP_S(J, SIMP(B), H)$
3. $J =$ "rA" where r is a number		
3.1 $r < 0$	Let $B \leftarrow INF_S(A, H)$	"rB"
3.2 $r \geq 0$	Let $B \leftarrow SUP_S(A, H)$	"rB"
4. $J =$ "$rv + A$" where r is a number, v a variable	Let $B \leftarrow SUP_S(A, H \bigcup \{v\})$	
4.1 v occurs in B	Let $C \leftarrow SIMP("rv + B")$	$SUP_S(C, H)$
4.2 v does not occur in B	Let $C \leftarrow SUP_S("rv", H)$	"$C + B$"
5. $J =$ "$\min(A, B)$"	Let $C \leftarrow SUP_S(A, H)$ $D \leftarrow SUP_S(B, H)$	"$\min(C, D)$"
6. $J =$ "$A + B$"	Let $C \leftarrow SUP_S(A, H)$ $D \leftarrow SUP_S(B, H)$	"$C + D$"
7. $J =$ "$\sin(A)$"		$TRIG_S(A, ' \sin, 'SUP)$
8. $J =$ "$\cos(A)$"		$TRIG_S(A, ' \cos, 'SUP)$
9. $J =$ "$1/A$"		
9.1 A has known parity	Let $B \leftarrow INF_S(A, H)$	"$1/B$"
9.2 A has unknown parity	Let $b \leftarrow INF_S(A, \emptyset)$ $c \leftarrow SUP_S(A, \emptyset)$	
9.2.1 $b > c$		$-\infty$
9.2.2 $bc > 0$		"$1/b$"
9.2.3 $bc \leq 0$		∞
10. $J =$ "$v^n A$" where v is a variable with known parity, not occurring in A, also of known parity		
10.1 A, J same parity	Let $B \leftarrow SUP_S(A, H \bigcup \{v\})$	
10.2 A, J opp. parity	Let $B \leftarrow INF_S(A, H \bigcup \{v\})$	
10.x.1 v occurs in B	Let $C \leftarrow SIMP("v^n B")$	$SUP_S(C, H)$
10.x.2 v, J same parity	Let $C \leftarrow SUP_S(v, H)$	"$C^n B$"
10.x.3 v, J opp. parity	Let $C \leftarrow INF_S(v, H)$	"$C^n B$"

Figure 5.1. Continued.

IF	ACTION	RETURN
11. $J =$ "AB" where A and B have known parity		
11.1 A, J same parity	Let $C \leftarrow \text{SUP}_S(A, H)$	
11.2 A, J opp. parity	Let $C \leftarrow \text{INF}_S(A, H)$	
11.x.1 B, J same parity	Let $D \leftarrow \text{SUP}_S(B, H)$	"CD"
11.x.2 B, J opp. parity	Let $D \leftarrow \text{INF}_S(B, H)$	"CD"
12. $J =$ "AB" where A has known parity, B has unknown	Let $c \leftarrow \text{INF}_S(B, \emptyset)$ $d \leftarrow \text{SUP}_S(B, \emptyset)$	
12.1 $0 \leq c$	Let $E \leftarrow \text{SUP}_S(A, H)$	
12.1.1 A positive		"dE"
12.1.2 A negative		"cE"
12.2 $d < 0$	Let $E \leftarrow \text{INF}_S(A, H)$	
12.2.1 A positive		"dE"
12.2.2 A negative		"cE"
12.3 $0 \leq d$		
12.3.1 A positive	Let $E \leftarrow \text{SUP}_S(A, H)$	"dE"
12.3.2 A negative	Let $E \leftarrow \text{INF}_S(A, H)$	"cE"
13. $J =$ "AB" where A and B have unknown parity	Let $c \leftarrow \text{INF}_S(A, \emptyset)$ $d \leftarrow \text{SUP}_S(A, \emptyset)$ $e \leftarrow \text{INF}_S(B, \emptyset)$ $f \leftarrow \text{SUP}_S(B, \emptyset)$	
13.1 $c > d$		$-\infty$
13.2 $e > f$		$-\infty$
13.3		$\max(ce, cf, de, df)$
14. $J =$ "$\sqrt{A}$"		
14.1 A positive	Let $B \leftarrow \text{SUP}_S(A, H)$	"$\sqrt{B}$"
14.2 A negative		$-\infty$
14.3 A has unknown parity		$-\infty$
15. $J =$ "$\text{arcsin}(A)$"	Let $a \leftarrow \text{SUP}_S(A, \emptyset)$	$\text{arcsin}(a)$
16.		$\text{SUPPP}_S(J, H)$

INF is defined exactly symmetrically to SUP above, with the following textual substitutions: SUP $\rightarrow$ INF, INF $\rightarrow$ SUP, SUPP $\rightarrow$ INFF, HIVAL $\rightarrow$ LOVAL, UPPER $\rightarrow$ LOWER, min $\rightarrow$ max, max $\rightarrow$ min, $\infty \rightarrow -\infty$ and $-\infty \rightarrow \infty$, except in the *action* columns of 12.1, 12.2 and 12.3, SUP and INF are not changed, while the inequalities in those *if* columns are reversed.

Figure 5.2. Definition of algorithm SUPP and lexical changes
needed to define algorithm INFF.

Algorithm $\text{SUPP}_S(x, Y, H)$

Iғ	Action	Return
1. x does not occur in Y		Y
2. $x = Y$		∞
3. $Y = \text{``min}(A, B)\text{''}$	Let $C \leftarrow \text{SUPP}_S(x, A, H)$ $D \leftarrow \text{SUPP}_S(x, B, H)$	$\text{``min}(C, D)\text{''}$
4. $Y = \text{``}bx + C\text{''}$ where b is a number, x does not occur in C		
4.1 $b > 1$		∞
4.2 $b < 1$		$\text{``}C/(1 - b)\text{''}$
4.3 $b = 1$		
4.3.1 C has unknown parity		∞
4.3.2 $C < 0$		$-\infty$
4.3.3 $C \geq 0$		∞
5.		$\text{SUPPP}_S(Y, H)$

INFF is defined exactly symmetrically to SUPP above, with the following textual substitutions: SUPP $\rightarrow$ INFF, SUPPP $\rightarrow$ INFFF, min $\rightarrow$ max, $\infty \rightarrow -\infty$ and $-\infty \rightarrow \infty$. Also the inequalities in 4.3.2 and 4.3.3 are reversed.

The double quote marks around expressions in the figures mean that the values of variables within their range should be substituted into the expression, but no evaluation should occur. Thus for instance if the value of variable A is symbol x, and that of B is the symbolic expression $y + 3 - x$, then the value of "$A + B$" is "$x + y + 3 - x$." In general in the definitions of the algorithms, lower case variables have single numbers or symbols as their values, while upper case letters may also have complete expressions as their values. The function SIMP refers to the algebraic simplifier described in section 5.3.1 above. More liberal use of SIMP does not affect the correctness of the algorithms, it merely decreases efficiency. The function TRIG is described in detail below.

Each algorithm is described as a table of condition-action-return triples. This follows the notation used by Bledsoe [13] to describe the first version of these procedures. The original implementation of these algorithms was in the production rule system that is used for prediction and interpretation within Acronym. Each step in the decision table was represented as a production

Figure 5.3. Definition of algorithm SUPPP and lexical changes
needed to define algorithm INFFF.

Algorithm SUPPP$_S(Y, H)$

I$_F$	A$_{CTION}$	R$_{ETURN}$
1. Y is a number		Y
2. Y is a variable		
2.1 $Y \in H$		Y
2.2 $Y \notin H$		HIVAL$_S(Y)$
3. $Y = $ "$A + B$"	Let $C \leftarrow$ SUPPP$_S(A, H)$	
	$D \leftarrow$ SUPPP$_S(B, H)$	"$C + D$"
4. $Y = $ "$\min(A, B)$"	Let $C \leftarrow$ SUPPP$_S(A, H)$	
	$D \leftarrow$ SUPPP$_S(B, H)$	"$\min(C, D)$"
5. $Y = $ "$1/A$" where A has		
known parity	Let $B \leftarrow$ INFFF$_S(A, H)$	"$1/B$"
6. $Y = $ "AB" where A and B have		
known parity		
6.1 Y, A same parity	Let $C \leftarrow$ SUPPP$_S(A, H)$	
6.2 Y, A opp. parity	Let $C \leftarrow$ INFFF$_S(A, H)$	
6.n.1 Y, B same parity	Let $D \leftarrow$ SUPPP$_S(B, H)$	"CD"
6.n.2 Y, B opp. parity	Let $D \leftarrow$ INFFF$_S(B, H)$	"CD"
7.		∞

INFFF is defined exactly symmetrically to SUPPP above, with the following textual substitutions:
SUPPP $\rightarrow$ INFFF, INFFF $\rightarrow$ SUPPP, HIVAL $\rightarrow$ LOVAL, min $\rightarrow$ max and $\infty \rightarrow -\infty$.

---

rule. However the algorithms are highly recursive, and the overhead of
"procedure" invocation for production rules made the algorithms very slow.
The algorithms were rewritten directly in MACLISP gaining significant
speedups. However even in the LISP environment, using different options for
the code for procedure invocation can change the running time of the
algorithms by a factor of four. This gives some indication of just how
recursion-intensive these algorithms are.

Algorithms SUP, INF, SUPP, and INFF are extensions to algorithms of
the same names given by Shostak [53]. Algorithms SUPPP and INFFF are
new (as is algorithm TRIG). The first five steps of our SUP and INF, minus
step 2.2, comprise Shostak's SUP and INF. The additional steps (6 through
16) handle nonlinearities. Our algorithms SUPP and INFF are identical to

those of Shostak, with the addition of a final step which invokes SUPPP or INFFF in the respective cases. For a set of linear constraints and a linear expression to bound, the above algorithms behave identically to those of Shostak.

Given a set of constraints S, and an expression E, $\text{SUP}_S\ (E,\ \emptyset)$ a lower bound.

The following descriptions give an intuitive feel for what each of algorithms SUP, SUPP, and SUPPP compute. Dual statements hold for INF, INFF, and INFFF, respectively. S is always a set of constraints and H a set of variables (i.e., quantifiers) which occur in S.

> $\text{SUP}_S\ (J,\ H)$: where J is a simplified (by SIMP) expression in variables constrained by S, returns an expression E in variables in H. In particular if $H = \emptyset$ then SUP returns a number. In general if numerical values are assigned to variables in H, and E evaluated for those assignments, then its value is an upper bound on the value achievable by expression J over the assignments in the satisfying set of S which have the same assignments as fixed for the variables in H.

> $\text{SUPP}_S\ (x,\ Y,\ H)$: where x is a variable, x is not in H, and Y is a simplified expression in variables in $H \cup \{x\}$, returns an upper bound for x, which is an expression in variables in H, and is computed by "solving" $x \leq Y$, e.g., solving $x \leq 9 - 2x$ yields an upper bound of 3 for x.

> $\text{SUPPP}_S\ (Y,\ H)$: where Y is a simplified expression, returns an upper bound on Y, as does SUP, but in general the bounds are weaker than those of SUP. Essentially SUP uses SUPPP when it hasn't got specific methods to handle Y.

Algorithm TRIG is called from both SUP and INF. It is invoked with three arguments, the first an expression, the second the symbol "sin" or "cos" and the third is the symbol SUP or INF. Implicitly it has a fourth argument S which is the constraint set. It takes lower and upper bounds on A using $\text{INF}_S(A, \emptyset)$ and $\text{SUP}_S(A,\ \emptyset)$, then finds the indicated bound on the indicated trigonometric function over that interval.

Consider the example of figure 5.4. The given constraints are $a \geq 2$, $b \geq 1$, and $ab \leq 4$. These are normalized by the procedure described in section 5.4.1. Then a trace of $\text{SUP}_S\ (a, \emptyset)$ is shown. It eventually returns 4 as an upper bound for a over the satisfying set C_S of constraint set S. In fact 4 is the maximum value which a can achieve on C_S.

Figure 5.5 demonstrates finding an upper bound for $a^2\ b$, by invoking $\text{SUP}_S\ (a^2\ b, \emptyset)$ which returns 16. Again, 16 is also the maximum value which can be achieved by $a^2 b$ over the satisfying set of S. In general SUP will not return the maximum value for an expression, merely an upper bound. Shostak [53] gives an example of a linear constraint set, and a linear expression to bound where it fails to return the maximum.

Bledsoe [13] and Shostak [53] proved a number of properties of the algorithms SUP and INF for sets of linear constraints, and linear expressions to be bound. The properties of interest to us are:

Figure 5.4. Example of algorithm SUP bounding a variable over
the satisfying set of a set of constraints.

Given constraints $a \geq 2$, $b \geq 1$ and $ab \leq 4$ the normalization procedure produces as
set S the constraints:

$$2 \leq a \qquad\qquad a \leq 4 \times 1/b$$
$$1 \leq b \qquad\qquad b \leq 4 \times 1/a$$

$\text{SUP}_S(a, \emptyset) =$

$\quad \text{SUPP}_S(a, \text{SIMP}(\text{SUP}_S(\text{UPPER}_S(a), \{a\})), \emptyset)$ Step 2.3

$\quad = \text{SUPP}_S(a, \text{SIMP}(\text{SUP}_S(\min(4, 4 \times 1/b), \{a\})), \emptyset)$

$\quad = \text{SUPP}_S(a, \text{SIMP}(\min(\text{SUP}_S(4, \{a\}), \text{SUP}_S(4 \times 1/b, \{a\}))), \emptyset)$ Step 5

$\qquad \text{SUP}_S(4, \{a\}) = 4$ Step 1

$\qquad \text{SUP}_S(4 \times 1/b, \{a\}) =$

$\qquad\qquad 4 \times \text{SUP}_S(1/b, \{a\})$ Step 3.2

$\qquad\qquad = 4 \times 1/\text{INF}_S(b, \{a\})$ Step 9.1

$\qquad\qquad = 4 \times 1/\text{INFF}_S(b, \text{SIMP}(\text{INF}_S(\text{LOWER}_S(b), \{a, b\})), \{a\})$ Step 2.3

$\qquad\qquad = 4 \times 1/\text{INFF}_S(b, \text{SIMP}(\text{INF}_S(1, \{a, b\})), \{a\})$

$\qquad\qquad = 4 \times 1/\text{INFF}_S(b, 1, \{a\})$ Step 1

$\qquad\qquad = 4 \times 1/1$ Step 1 of INFF

$\quad = \text{SUPP}_S(a, \text{SIMP}(\min(4, 4 \times 1/1), \emptyset)$

$\quad = \text{SUPP}_S(a, 4, \emptyset)$

$\quad = 4$ Step 1 of SUPP

Figure 5.5. Example of algorithm SUP bounding a nonlinear
expression subject to a set of nonlinear constraints.

$\text{SUP}_S(a^2 b, \emptyset) =$

$\quad \text{Let } B = \text{SUP}_S(b, \{a\})$ Step 10.1

$\quad = \text{SUPP}_S(b, \text{SIMP}(\text{SUP}_S(\text{UPPER}_S(b), \{b, a\})), \{a\})$ Step 2.3

$\quad = \text{SUPP}_S(b, \text{SIMP}(\text{SUP}_S(\min(2, 4 \times 1/a), \{b, a\})), \{a\})$

$\quad = \text{SUPP}_S(b, \text{SIMP}(\min(\text{SUP}_S(2, \{b, a\}),$

$\qquad\qquad\qquad\qquad \text{SUP}_S(4 \times 1/a, \{b, a\}))), \{a\})$ Step 5

$\qquad \text{SUP}_S(2, \{b, a\}) = 2$ Step 1

$\qquad \text{SUP}_S(4 \times 1/a, \{b, a\}) =$

$\qquad\qquad 4 \times \text{SUP}_S(1/a, \{b, a\})$ Step 3.2

$\qquad\qquad = 4 \times 1/\text{INF}_S(a, \{b, a\})$ Step 9.1

$\qquad\qquad = 4 \times 1/a$ Step 2.1

$\quad = \text{SUPP}_S(b, \text{SIMP}(\min(2, 4 \times 1/a)), \{a\})$

$\quad = \text{SUPP}_S(b, \min(2, 4 \times 1/a), \{a\})$

$\quad = \min(2, 4 \times 1/a)$ Step 1 of SUPP

$\quad = \text{SUP}_S(\text{SIMP}(a^2 \min(2, 4 \times 1/a)), \emptyset)$ Step 10.x.1

$\quad = \text{SUP}_S(\min(2a^2, 4a), \emptyset)$

$\quad = \min(\text{SUP}_S(2a^2, \emptyset), \text{SUP}_S(4a, \emptyset))$ Step 5

$\qquad \text{SUP}_S(2a^2, \emptyset) =$

$\qquad\qquad 2 \times \text{SUP}_S(a^2, \emptyset)$ Step 3.2

$\qquad\qquad \text{Let } B = \text{SUP}_S(1, \{a\})$ Step 10.1

$\qquad\qquad = 1$ Step 1

$\qquad\qquad = 2 \times (\text{SUP}_S(a, \emptyset))^2$ Step 10.x.2

$\qquad\qquad = 2 \times 4^2$ as in fig. 5.4

$\qquad \text{SUP}_S(4a, \emptyset) =$

$\qquad\qquad 4 \times \text{SUP}_S(a, \emptyset)$ Step 3.2

$\qquad\qquad = 4 \times 4$ as in fig. 5.4

$\quad = \min(2 \times 4^2, 4 \times 4)$

$\quad = 16$

P1.   The algorithms terminate.

P2.   The algorithms return upper and lower bounds on expressions.

P3.   When the expression is a variable, and the auxiliary set (H in the notation above) is empty, the algorithms return a maximum and minimum (including $\pm\infty$ when appropriate).

The proofs of P1 and P2 (due to Bledsoe [13]) can be extended to the above algorithms.

First note that algorithms SUPPP and INFFF terminate, since all recursive calls reduce the number of symbols in their first argument, and they exit simply when the argument is a single symbol—via steps 1 or 2. By induction they return upper and lower bounds on their first argument. Essentially the algorithms evaluate their first argument at a vertex of a rectangloid which bounds the satisfying set of S. The rectangloid is determined by the numeric upper and lower bounds in the constraint set (as determined by HIVAL, LOVAL). If a term can't be shown to achieve its extreme value at a vertex of the projection of the rectangloid into the subspace of the variables of the term, then a most pessimistic estimate is used for its value; namely $\pm\infty$.

Algorithms SUPP and INFF are identical to those of Shostak [53], except that they can take more complex arguments, in which case they invoke SUPPP and INFFF, respectively, so from Bledsoe's proof, and argument above, they, too, terminate and provide appropriate bounds. Note that the overall performance of the constraint manipulation system may be improved by including extra techniques in SUPP and INFF to solve some nonlinear inequalities, rather than passing the bounding expressions to SUPPP and INFFF in those cases.

The proof that SUP and INF terminate follows that of Bledsoe [13], and all but steps 9.2, 12, 13, and 15 can be so covered (step 16 is covered by the arguments above for SUPPP and INFFF). The problem with these steps is that they reset the auxiliary set to be empty, so there is the danger of infinite recursion, where an identical call is made further down the computation tree. But all of these steps make recursive calls with first arguments containing fewer symbols. The only place the number of symbols can grow is step 2.3, and there the first argument is a single variable. Since there are only a finite number of pairs consisting of a variable, and a subset of the variables, any infinite recursion must include an infinite recursion on some form $\text{SUP}_S (v, H)$, and similarly for INF. But step 2.2 explicitly checks for duplication of such calls on the execution stack, so step 2.3 will not be reached (note that it is not sufficient to check for duplications of calls of the form $\text{SUP}_S (v, \emptyset)$ because steps 4 and 10, besides 2.3, can also increase the size of set H). That SUP and INF bound their first argument is a straightforward extension of the proof of Bledsoe [13].

Finally, note that many of the recursive calls to SUP and INF are of the form SUP_S $(v, \emptyset)$ for some variable v. Each such evaluation generates a large computation tree. Therefore the algorithms are modified in their implementations to check for this case explicitly. The first time such a call is made for a given set S, the result is compared to the numeric bound on the variable v amongst the constraints in S (as indexed with function HIVAL— recall the normal form for constraint sets). If the calculated bound is better, then S is changed to reflect this. Subsequent invocations of SUP_S $(v, \emptyset)$ on an unchanged S simply use HIVAL to retrieve the previously calculated result. This is similar to the notion of a memo function as described by Michie [43].

5.4.3 A Partial Decision Procedure

Now the partial decision procedure used by ACRONYM's CMS can be described. It is completely analogous to that used by Bledsoe and Shostak.

If for each variable (quantifier) x, constrained by a constraint set S, it is true that:

$$INF_S(\text{``}x\text{''}, \emptyset) \leq SUP_S (\text{``}x\text{''}, \emptyset)$$

then S said to be *possibly satisfiable*, otherwise it is *definitely unsatisfiable*.

As an example suppose that the constraint $b \geq 1$ is changed to $b \geq 3$ in the example of figure 5.4. Then the bounds derived for a and b using INF and SUP are:

$$2 \leq a \leq 1.333$$
$$3 \leq b \leq 2$$

So the decision procedure concludes that the constraints are definitely not satisfiable. Note also that for these constraints INF produces a larger lower bound for a^2b than the upper bound produced by SUP.

The soundness of the partial decision procedure follows directly from the fact that for a satisfiable set S, SUP and INF return upper and lower bounds on expressions over that set (for soundness it is not necessary that they return least upper bounds and greatest lower bounds).

However a partial decision procedure that always returned the same result, namely that the constraint set is *possibly satisfiable* is also sound. A partial decision procedure is only interesting if it sometimes detects unsatisfiable sets of constraints. The more often it successfully detects such sets, the more interesting it is.

I do not have a good characterization of what classes of inconsistent constraints the CMS can detect. In practice no cases have been encountered where it has failed to detect an inconsistency. I hypothesize that for sets of linear constraints the CMS is in fact a full decision procedure. I further hypothesize that for sets of constraints free of sines and cosines, and where every term has known parity, the CMS is also a full decision procedure. It is possible to construct inconsistent constraints which it cannot decide are unsatisfiable.

Finally it should be pointed out that the decision procedure can be augmented by checking that the intervals estimated for a quantifier which is known to be an integer—e.g., it represents the number of some type of subparts—can be checked to see whether they include an integer. If not, the set S can be rejected as unsatisfiable.

5.4.4 Approximating Complex Expressions

After implementing the CMS described in the previous section, it was realized that the functions involved had some useful applications which had not been anticipated.

Since the partial decision procedure is at least exponential in the number of symbols in the constraint set, it is desirable to keep the constraint set simple when possible. Informally, at least, it also seems that inclusion of expressions involving cos, sin, or simply expression of indeterminate parity is expensive, as analysis of bounds on these expressions using SUP and INF involve "resetting" of the argument H to the empty set $\emptyset$, making the invocation tree even deeper. Thus while Taylor [58] was interested in linearizing expressions so they could be handled with the simplex method, ACRONYM needs to approximate expressions with simpler expressions with fewer symbols, and perhaps free of nonmonotonic subexpressions.

The algorithms SUP and INF prove to be extremely useful for precisely this task. By invoking them with a nonempty set H of variables, expressions in just those variables in H are returned, which are respectively upper and lower bounds on the given expression over the satisfying set of the constraint set. More formally, given an expression E, a set of variables H, and a set of constraints S then $\text{INF}_S(E, H)$ and $\text{SUP}_S(E, H)$ are expressions involving only variables in H and

$$\text{INF}_S(E, H) \leq E \leq \text{SUP}_S(E, H)$$

is true identically over the satisfying set of S.

Two examples of bounding expressions by simpler expressions will be given.

The first arises during the prediction phases of the aircraft example given in chapter 9. The predictor finds an expression of the height of the camera above one of the wings of the aircraft as

$$h = -\text{HEIGHT} - 0.667 \times \text{FUSELAGE-RADIUS.}$$

The predictor decides for various reasons explained in chapter 7 that quantifier FUSELAGE-RADIUS is insignificant in this expression, relative to the HEIGHT term. It uses algorithms SUP and INF to remove FUSELAGE-RADIUS from the expression for h and determine upper and lower bounds as functions of HEIGHT.

Given a constraint set S including the following constraints:

$$2.5 \leq \text{FUSELAGE-RADIUS} \leq 4.0$$
$$1000 \leq \quad \text{HEIGHT} \quad \leq 12000$$

then INF_S *(h, {HEIGHT})* produces a lower bound of:

$$-2.667 - \text{HEIGHT}$$

and SUP_S *(h, {HEIGHT})* gives:

$$-1.667 - \text{HEIGHT}$$

as an upper bound.

The second example will be used further in the next section (i.e. section 5.5). There are a number of variables expressing errors in the position and location of a box, a manipulator hand, and the orientation of a screw on the end of a screwdriver. It is desired to find upper and lower bounds on the expression Δy in terms of a single quantifier DRIVER-LENGTH where Δy is given by:

$\Delta y = - 1.260 - 1.516 \times \sin(\text{BOX-DELTA-ORI})$
$\quad - 1.25 \times \sin(\text{HAND-WOBBLE-Y}) \times \sin(\text{SCREW-WOBBLE-Z})$
$\quad \times \sin(-\text{HAND-WOBBLE-X})$
$\quad \times \sin(\text{BOX-DELTA-ORI} + \text{HAND-WOBBLE-Z})$
$\quad - \text{BOX-DELTA-POS-Y} \times \cos(\text{BOX-DELTA-ORI})$
$\quad - \text{HAND-DELTA-POS-X} \times \sin(\text{BOX-DELTA-ORI})$
$\quad + 1.25 \times \cos(\text{HAND-WOBBLE-Y}) \times \cos(\text{SCREW-WOBBLE-Z})$
$\quad \times \sin(\text{SCREW-WOBBLE-Y})$
$\quad \times \sin(\text{BOX-DELTA-ORI} + \text{HAND-WOBBLE-Z})$
$\quad + 1.25 \times \cos(\text{SCREW-WOBBLE-Y}) \times \cos(\text{SCREW-WOBBLE-Z})$
$\quad \times \cos(-\text{HAND-WOBBLE-X}) \times \sin(\text{HAND-WOBBLE-Y})$
$\quad \times \sin(\text{BOX-DELTA-ORI} + \text{HAND-WOBBLE-Z})$
$\quad + 1.25 \times \cos(\text{SCREW-WOBBLE-Y}) \times \cos(\text{SCREW-WOBBLE-Z})$
$\quad \times \cos(\text{BOX-DELTA-ORI} + \text{HAND-WOBBLE-Z})$
$\quad \times \sin(-\text{HAND-WOBBLE-X})$

+ 1.25 × cos(-HAND-WOBBLE-X)
  × cos(BOX-DELTA-ORI + HAND-WOBBLE-Z)
  × sin(SCREW-WOBBLE-Z)
+ 1.260 × cos(BOX-DELTA-ORI)
+ BOX-DELTA-POS-X × sin(BOX-DELTA-ORI)
+ DRIVER-LENGTH × cos(-HAND-WOBBLE-X)
  × sin(HAND-WOBBLE-Y)
  × DRIVER-LENGTH
  × cos(BOX-DELTA-ORI + HAND-WOBBLE-Z)
  × sin(-HAND-WOBBLE-X)
+ HAND-DELTA-POS-Y × cos(BOX-DELTA-ORI)

The quantifiers are well constrained by

-0.05	≤	BOX-DELTA-POS-X	≤	0.05
-0.05	≤	BOX-DELTA-POS-Y	≤	0.05
-0.5°	≤	BOX-DELTA-ORI	≤	0.5°
-0.05	≤	HAND-DELTA-POS-X	≤	0.05
-0.05	≤	HAND-DELTA-POS-Y	≤	0.05
-0.25°	≤	HAND-WOBBLE-X	≤	0.25°
-0.05°	≤	HAND-WOBBLE-Y	≤	0.25°
-0.25°	≤	HAND-WOBBLE-Z	≤	0.25°
-2°	≤	SCREW-WOBBLE-Y	≤	2°
-2°	≤	SCREW-WOBBLE-Z	≤	2°

and DRIVER-LENGTH is known to be positive. The CMS is able to deduce that:

$$-0.164 - 0.00442039 \times \text{DRIVER\_LENGTH} \leq$$
$$\Delta y \leq 0.164 + 0.00442042 \times \text{DRIVER\_LENGTH}.$$

5.5 An Example from Planning

This section demonstrates a possible use of the constraint system in planning for manipulator tasks. An example taken from Taylor [58] is used. His results are duplicated and extended significantly from numeric to symbolic bounds. This extention opens up new avenues for making use of algebraic and geometric constraints in planning. In the example, constraints are derived on tool selection by considering the effects of the tool parameters on position and orientation errors in an insertion task.

Figure 5.6 is a close-up view of an ACRONYM model of the situation described in example 2 of appendix E of Taylor [58]. Appendix A1 section

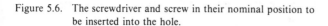
Figure 5.6.   The screwdriver and screw in their nominal position to
              be inserted into the hole.

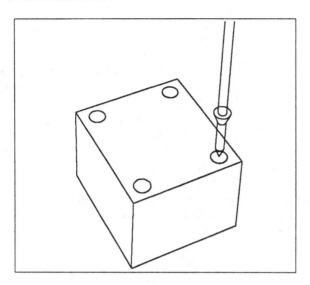

A1.3 of this study contains the details of the model specification given to
ACRONYM in order to generate the figure and carry out the analysis below.

There is a box with four holes in its top sitting on a table with a given
position and orientation about the vertical axis. The position and orientation
are subject to known errors. A manipulator hand holding a screwdriver, with
a screw at the end, is placed above one of the holes. It has three degrees of
position error and three degrees of orientation error. In addition, the screw
has two degrees of rotational freedom in its attachment to the screwdriver. It
can wobble backwards and forwards about two orthogonal axes which go
through the center of the end of the screwdriver shaft. If all errors in position
and orientation are zero then the tip of the screw should be exactly in the
center of the hole on the box. Such a situation is illustrated in figure 5.6.

Taylor was interested in predicting the error in the location of the tip of
the screw relative to the center of the hole. ACRONYM can do this easily by
tracing through the affixment tree to get a symbolic expression for the
coordinates of the screw-tip in the coordinate system of the whole. It
multiplies out the coordinate transforms symbolically to get expressions for
the three coordinates. With zero errors these coordinates would be $(0, 0, 0)$.
The ranges of possible values for the three coordinates indicate the position
errors in the placement of the screw-tip. The last example in the previous
section used an expression for Δy. This is exactly the expression ACRONYM
obtains for the y-coordinate. The other coordinates are given by expressions
of similar complexity.

Taylor used the following constraints on the errors. The quantifier names are indicative of the errors to which they refer.

–0.3	≤	BOX-DELTA-POS-X	≤	0.3
–0.2	≤	BOX-DELTA-POS-Y	≤	0.2
–5°	≤	BOX-DELTA-ORI	≤	5°
–0.05	≤	HAND-DELTA-POS-X	≤	0.05
–0.05	≤	HAND-DELTA-POS-Y	≤	0.05
–0.25°	≤	HAND-WOBBLE-X	≤	0.25°
–0.25°	≤	HAND-WOBBLE-Y	≤	0.25°
–0.25°	≤	HAND-WOBBLE-Z	≤	0.25°
–5°	≤	SCREW-WOBBLE-Y	≤	5°
–5°	≤	SCREW-WOBBLE-Z	≤	5°

Taylor used a screwdriver length DRIVER-LENGTH of exactly 10 inches.

Algorithms SUP and INF were applied to the coordinate expressions, resulting in the following bounds:

$$-0.0607 \leq \Delta x \leq 0.0510$$
$$-0.590 \leq \Delta y \leq 0.585$$
$$-0.660 \leq \Delta z \leq 0.654$$

where $+x$ is the direction down the hole (note that this is a different coordinate system to that used by Taylor). These bounds compare with those obtained by Taylor:

$$-0.05 \leq \Delta x \leq 0.05$$
$$-0.54 \leq \Delta y \leq 0.54$$
$$-0.62 \leq \Delta z \leq 0.62$$

The differences between Taylor's estimates and ACRONYM's (though small) can be attributed to two factors. Taylor linearizes products of rotations with a differential approximation. This works well for very small rotations, but it tends to ignore the effect of applying the second rotation to the perturbation introduced by the first. With rotations of magnitude up to 5° as in this example the errors in this approximation can start to make a difference in the computed values. The second source of difference between Taylor's and ACRONYM's estimates is due to the poor bounding behavior of the CMS on sums of trigonometric terms. While ACRONYM makes no linear approximations, and instead considers all trigonometric terms, the bounding algorithms treat them independently and may miss cancellations of errors between coupled terms. Much of the power of the CMS is wasted as all the variables (each an error estimate) are independent.

Note however that ACRONYM's error *over estimates* are not much larger than Taylor's *under estimates*.

Furthermore, since ACRONYM's techniques are more symbolic than Taylor's (he uses the simplex method as his main computational tool), it is possible to ask a much richer class of questions concerning the implications of the geometry and the constraints.

Suppose, for instance, that the insertion task illustrated in figure 5.6 is to be achieved by applying a downward force, compliant about the screw tip, using either a passive compliance device (e.g., Drake [23]) or active dynamic control (e.g., Salisbury [51]). Then it is sufficient that the tip of the screw falls somewhere in the top of the open hole. Note that the hole opening is the size of the head of the screw rather than the size of the screw shaft. Compliant motion will guide the screw into its correctly seated position. This constraint can be expressed by

$$\sqrt{(\Delta y)^2 + (\Delta z)^2} \leq 0.25$$

where the hole opening has radius 0.25 inches. Since algorithms SUPP and INFF currently solve only linear equations and not quadratics, and since the errors in the y and z coordinates are essentially independent, it is simpler in this case to approximate the above constraint with the following two:

$$-0.25 \sqrt{0.5} \leq \Delta y \leq 0.25 \sqrt{0.5}$$
$$-0.25 \sqrt{0.5} \leq \Delta z \leq 0.25 \sqrt{0.5}$$

These constraints can be used to assist in automatic plan generation of the insertion task. The following example uses a tighter set of constraints than those used by Taylor on errors in placement of the box. The box placement errors he used tend to swamp any other errors. A smaller amount of wobble in the attachment of the screw to the screwdriver is also assumed. The actual values used are the constraints given at the end of the previous section (sec. 5.4.4). It is further presumed that the screwdriver length is not predetermined—i.e. there are a number of screwdrivers of different lengths available for use. The plan generated must include selection of one for this task.

Let A be the set of quantifiers which can be changed in the plan, and let S be the set of constraints on all quantifiers. Typically A might include the screwdriver length and nominal positions and orientations of the box, but exclude the error quantifiers. The above constraints can then be translated to the following.

$$-0.25 \sqrt{0.5} \leq INF_S(\Delta y, A) \qquad\qquad SUP_S(\Delta y, A) \leq 0.25 \sqrt{0.5}$$
$$-0.25 \sqrt{0.5} \leq INF_S(\Delta z, A) \qquad\qquad SUP_S(\Delta z, A) \leq 0.25 \sqrt{0.5}$$

In this case the only quantifier in A which appears in the expressions for Δy and Δz is DRIVER-LENGTH and each of the above inequalities results in a linear constraint on that quantifier. The previous section 5.4.4 demonstrated finding the bounds on Δy for this example. The result is

$$-0.25 \sqrt{0.5} \leq -0.164 - 0.004420 \times \text{DRIVER-LENGTH}$$
$$0.164 + 0.004420 \times \text{DRIVER-LENGTH} \leq 0.25 \sqrt{0.5}$$
$$-0.25 \sqrt{0.5} \leq -0.162 - 0.004204 \times \text{DRIVER-LENGTH}$$
$$0.162 + 0.004204 \times \text{DRIVER-LENGTH} \leq 0.25 \sqrt{0.5}$$

which gives for instance that

$$\text{DRIVER-LENGTH} \leq 2.92$$

If the new constraints are inconsistent with the constraints already in the set S, then either the current plan is unworkable or the bounds found by SUP and INF were poor. Thus the planning system must be careful of the tasks it gives the CMS, being careful not to overtax it, so that its conclusions can be used confidently to redirect the planning effort when the CMS indicates an unworkable plan.

6

Geometric Reasoning

Geometric reasoning is making deductions about spatial relationships of objects in three dimensions given some description of their positions, orientations, and shapes. There are many straightforward, and some not-so-straightforward, ways to calculate properties of spatial relationships numerically when situations are completely specified. Given the generic classes of objects that are modeled in ACRONYM and generic positions and orientations that ACRONYM's representation admits, purely numerical techniques are obviously inadequate.

A number of other workers have faced similar problems in the area of planning manipulation tasks. The next section compares briefly a few of their solutions to these problems below. They can be characterized as applying analytic algebraic tools to geometry. That is the general approach taken in ACRONYM. It deals with more general situations however. There are other approaches to these problems; most rely on simplifying the descriptive terms to coarse predicates. However, then deductive results must necessarily be similarly unrefined in nature.

Section 6.3 deals with algorithms for algebraic simplification of geometric expressions. Such simplifications are at the core of ACRONYM's geometric reasoning capabilities. Chapter 7 shows how they are used during prediction.

6.1 Approaches

Ambler and Popplestone [4] assume they are given a description of a goal state of spatial relationships between a set of objects, such as "against" and "fits," and describe a system for determining the relative positions and orientations of objects which satisfy these relations. The method assumes that there are at least two distinct expressions for relative positions and orientations derivable from the constraints. These are equated to give a geometric equation. They then use a simplifier for geometric expressions which can handle a subset of that of the system described below in section 6.3. Finally they use special purpose techniques to solve the small class of simplified equations that can be produced from the problems which can be handled by the system. The solution may retain degrees of freedom.

Lozano-Pérez [37] attacks a similar problem, but with more restrictions on the relationships specifiable. He is therefore able to use simpler methods to solve cases where there are no variations allowed in parameters. He describes a method for extending this to cases where parameters can vary over an interval by propagating those intervals through the constraints. He relies on strong restrictions on the allowed class of geometric situations for this to work.

Taylor [58] tackles a problem similar to ours. He has positions and locations of objects represented as parameterized coordinate transforms, and looks for bounds on the position coordinates of objects, given constraints on the parameters. An incomplete set of rules is used to simplify transform expressions as much as possible, based on the constraints. Then if only one rotational degree of freedom remains, the transform is expanded into explicit coordinate expressions that are linearized by assuming small errors. The simplex method is used to estimate bounds on these expressions.

McDermott [42] describes a representational scheme for metric relations between fairly unstructured objects in a planar map. Coordinates and orientations within and between frames of reference are represented by ranges. A multidimensional indexing scheme (based on k-d trees) is used to answer questions involving near neighbors of objects which satisfy additional constraints. The system has mostly been used for planning paths past incompletely specified obstacles. The ACRONYM constraint manipulation system (chap. 5) and the ACRONYM geometric simplifier described below are together able to make stronger deductions than those described by McDermott.

6.2 Geometric Reasoning in ACRONYM

In the ACRONYM context, there are spatial relationships among objects themselves, and a camera frame, which are not specified at all directly. Typically it is necessary to combine more than 10 coordinate transforms, involving 4 or more variables (quantifiers) to determine relative positions and orientations of coordinate frames. There are two primary requirements for ACRONYM's geometric reasoning system.

1. Identify observables that an object will generate and find characterizations of them which are invariant over the modeled range of variations. The system is given an expression in many variables for the position and orientation of the object relative to the camera frame, and given a set of constraints on those variables (encapsulated in a restriction node).

Here an *observable* is an image feature which will be detected and described by the image description processes. Observables with such invariant characterizations are called *quasi-invariant observables*.

    2. Discover further constraints which can be used to split the range of variations into cases in which further quasi-invariant observables can be predicted.

As a by-product of achieving the above objectives, ways are gained of using measurements of image features to deduce three-dimensional information. From the example of section 5.5 it is clear that the techniques developed here for geometric reasoning will be useful in planning manipulation tasks, based on an ACRONYM-style representation of generic spatial relationships.

Figure 6.1.   Two views of the electric screwdriver in its holder. The left is from a camera a little above the table, with variable pan and tilt. The right is from a camera directly above the table with variable pitch and roll.

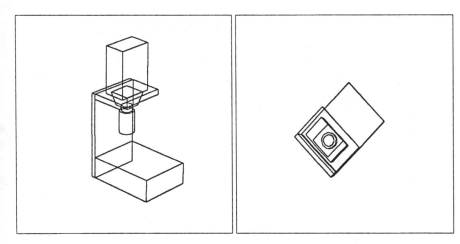

Throughout this chapter and the next, the two situations shown in figure 6.1 are used as examples. These are two views, with different camera geometries, of the same electric screwdriver sitting in its holder (it is one of the tools used by the manipulator arms in Stanford's coordinated robotics experimental work station). The position is represented by the quantifier SH_X inches in the *x* direction of table (world) coordinates and SH_Y inches in the *y* direction. Its orientation is a rotation about the vertical *z*-axis in world coordinates of magnitude SH_ORI. The following constraints apply to the position quantifiers:

$$0 \leq SH\_X \leq 24$$
$$18 \leq SH\_Y \leq 42$$

The orientation SH_ORI is unconstrained.

In the left situation of figure 6.1 the camera is at world coordinates (83.5, 30, 25) with variable pan and tilt represented by the quantifiers PAN and TILT. The following constraints apply:

$$\pi/12 \leq TILT \leq \pi/6$$
$$-\pi/12 \leq PAN \leq \pi/12$$

Setting TILT and PAN to zero corresponds to the camera looking along a ray parallel to, but opposite in direction to, the world x-axis. The camera is a couple of feet above the table, tilted slightly downwards, looking at the screwdriver and its holder about five to seven feet away.

The right-hand diagram of figure 6.1 is a view from an overhead camera at world coordinates (24, 30, HEIGHT), where HEIGHT is a constrained quantifier (the uncertainty in the height of the camera may make this example seem a little contrived; it is meant to be illustrative in nature). The camera image plane is rotated about the y and x axes with magnitudes represented by the quantifiers PITCH and ROLL respectively. The following constraints apply:

$$-\pi/12 \leq PITCH \leq \pi/12$$
$$-\pi/12 \leq ROLL \leq \pi/12$$
$$60 \leq HEIGHT \leq 84$$

Section 6.3 shows how to simplify large products of coordinate transforms using some identities which allow rotations to be transposed within a rotation product expression. Simplification of the coordinate transforms relating objects to each other and to the camera allows us to decide whether objects are in the field of view and what objects might be expected to occlude others. The simplified expressions are in a form which allows for prediction of invariant and quasi-invariant features. In particular they can be used in the prediction of the projected two-dimensional image shape of objects.

6.3 Geometric Simplification

The *geometric simplifier* takes a symbolic product of coordinate transforms and produces a single coordinate transform which is a pair of expressions for a rotation and a translation by using the following identity (recall the notation from chap. 4):

$$(R_1, T_1) * (R_2, T_2) = (R_1 * R_2, R_1 \otimes T_2 + T_1) \qquad (6.1)$$

The rotation expression obtained is thus a product of rotations. Using distributivity of rotations over translations, the translation expression becomes a sum of terms, each of which is a product of rotations applied to a vector.

The expressions in the coordinate transform are simplified to *standard forms*. Equivalent expressions will not necessarily be reduced to the same standard expression. The noncanonical nature of the reduction methods is not due only to the fact that the algebraic simplifier they use does not produce a canonical form. It is inherent in the methods themselves. Similar arguments to those of de Kleer and Sussman [34] apply to this case also. If the mechanisms which use the simplified geometric expressions are intelligent about their use and are robust in the face of occasional failure to identify a product of rotations as the identity, for instance, then the utility of a natural standard form, which is not necessarily canonical, far outweighs the benefits of having a canonical form which may be clumsy in expression and may be expensive in time and space to compute.

The geometric simplification mechanisms used by ACRONYM are useful because of certain inherent properties of cultural artifacts. Some such properties are stated here, but no empirical evidence is provided for them. Suppose the objects in a human-built setting have been described by generalized cones in a "natural" way. By that it is meant that for a given generalized cone, the spine (the *x*-axis of its coordinate system) lies along an axis of generalized translational invariance [10], and that if the cross section has an axis of generalized symmetry then that corresponds to one of the other coordinate axes of the cone's coordinate system. Then given two mechanically coupled cones (whether attached or merely coincident in some way), frequently their coordinate systems will have a pair of parallel axes (e.g., the *x*-axis of one may be parallel to the *z*-axis of the other). Furthermore it will often be the case that there are two (and hence three) pairs of parallel axes.

One approach to geometric simplification is to turn all rotation expressions into three by three matrices involving sine and cosine terms, multiply them out, then use an algebraic simplifier. (Similar approaches use homogeneous coordinates; the same arguments apply.) That course is not followed for two reasons. First it means that the algebraic simplifier must search for trigonometric simplifications that are obscure in the expanded form, but obvious in the unexpanded geometric notation, both due to the abundance of the spatial relations described in the previous paragraph, and due to the simple algebraic relation in axis-magnitude representation between a rotation and its inverse. Second, as is shown in section 7.2, better use can be made of expressions describing spatial relations as combinations of simple geometric transforms than could be made of a single rotation and translation expression, where the axis and magnitude of the rotation are both complex trigonometric forms.

6.3.1 Products of Rotations

Rotations of three space form a group under composition. The group is associative so it is permissible to simplify a symbolic product of rotations by collapsing adjacent ones with algebraically equal axis expressions (recall that rotations are represented as magnitudes about an axis) by adding their magnitudes. The group is not commutative, however. It is not possible to merely collect all rotations with common axis expressions. There is a slightly weaker condition on the elements of the group which allows partial use of this idea. Let a_1 and a_2 be vectors, and m_1 and m_2 be scalars. Then the following two identities are true (the proof is simple but tedious and omitted here):

$$(a_1, \ m_1) * (a_2, \ m_2) = (a_2, \ m_2) * (((a_2, \ - \ m_2) \otimes a_1), \ m_1)$$
$$(a_1, \ m_1) * (a_2, \ m_2) = (((a_1, \ m_1) \otimes a_2), \ m_2) * (a_1, \ m_1)$$

The geometric reasoning system of Ambler and Popplestone [4] collapses adjacent rotations sharing common axis expressions and uses the special case of the above identities where $a_1 = \hat{x}$, $a_2 = \hat{y}$ and $m_2 = \pi$ to simplify geometric expressions.

A special case, more general than that used by Ambler and Popplestone, is used here (and the general case in parts of the system—see chap. 7) to "shift" rotations to the left and right in the product expression. However, as a rotation is shifted it leaves rotations with complex axis expressions in its wake. There is a subgroup of rotations for which these axis expressions are no more complex than the originals. This is the group of 24 rotations which permute the positive and negative x, y, and z axes among themselves. When they are used with the above identities, the new axis expression is a permutation of the original axis components, perhaps with some sign changes.

Notice that these rotations are precisely the ones which relate two coordinate systems with two (or three) parallel pairs of axes; they are very common in models of human-made objects. Of particular interest is a generating subset of this rotational subgroup. It consists of the identity rotation *i*, and rotations about the three coordinate axes whose magnitudes are multiples of $\pi/2$. They are written as x_1, x_2, x_3, y_1, y_2, y_3, z_1, z_2, and z_3. The subscript indicates the magnitude of the rotation as a multiple of $\pi/2$. These 10 rotations are called *elementary*. The 15 other axis preserving rotations can not be expressed as rotations about a coordinate axis, but they can be expressed as a product of at most 2 elementary rotations. Furthermore they can be pictured intuitively by someone modeling an object, so they tend to be the most common way in which users describe orientations to ACRONYM. They tend to occur in relating parts of an object to one another.

Since in general $(-a, m) = (a, -m)$, elementary rotations are closed under inverses (negation of the magnitude) and under the identities given above. For instance:

$$x_3 * y_1 = y_1 * z_3$$
$$x_3 * y_1 = z_3 * x_3$$

A rotation is called *principal* if its axis is in the direction of one of the coordinate axes. These were the other type of rotation that were mentioned above as commonly occurring in models of human-made objects. Elementary rotations map $\hat{x}$, $\hat{y}$, and $\hat{z}$ among themselves and their negations, so using the two identities, it is seen that moving an elementary rotation past a principal rotation, either to the left or the right, leaves another principal rotation in its wake. For example:

$$(\hat{x}, m) * y_1 = y_1 * (\hat{z}, m)$$
$$y_1 * (\hat{x}, m) = (\hat{x}, -m) * y_1$$

Products of rotations which include elementary rotations are simplified by transposing using the identities above and multiplying out adjacent elementary and adjacent principal rotations which share the same axis. Consider the following five simplification rules:

SR1: Compose adjacent elementary or adjacent principal rotations sharing the same axis of rotation, and remove all instances of the identity rotation.

SR2: Move instances of z_1, z_2 and z_3 to the left of the expression and apply SR1.

SR3: While there is an *x*-axis elementary rotation in the expression which is not right-most, choose the left-most such, move it one place to the right and apply SR2.

SR4: While there is a y-axis elementary rotation in the expression which is not right-most or immediately to the left of an x-axis elementary rotation, move it to the right one place and apply SR1.

SR5: Make substitutions at the right of the expression using the following identities and apply SR2:

$$y_1 * x_1 = z_3 * y_1, \quad y_1 * x_2 = z_2 * y_1, \quad y_1 * x_3 = z_1 * y_1$$
$$y_2 * x_1 = z_2 * x_3, \quad y_2 * x_2 = i \quad\quad y_2 * x_3 = z_2 * x_1$$
$$y_3 * x_1 = z_1 * y_3, \quad y_3 * x_2 = z_2 * y_3, \quad y_3 * x_3 = z_3 * y_3$$

If these are applied to a symbolic product of rotations, then after applying each of the five rules in order, the expression contains at most two elementary rotations. Any such elementary rotations will either be left-most and one of z_1, z_2 or z_3, or will be right-most and one of x_1, x_2, x_3, y_1, or y_3.

To show that the five rules do indeed produce such a standard form is straightforward. The only potential difficulty is in showing the termination of SR3, since at each step the application of SR2 may produce an x-axis elementary rotation left of that which was previously left-most. Observe however that if z_e and x_e are elementary z-axis and x-axis rotations respectively, and $w * z_e = z_e * x_e$, then w must be an elementary y-axis rotation. Using this, termination follows from showing that the number of elementary rotations in the expression, apart from a left-most z-axis elementary rotation, is reduced by one at each phase of SR3.

The following expression is the "raw" product of rotations expressing the orientation of the screwdriver *tool* (the only cylinder in the left-hand illustration of fig. 6.1) relative to the camera. It was obtained by inverting the rotation expression for the camera relative to world coordinates and composing that with the expression for the orientation of the *tool* in world coordinates, found by tracing down the affixment tree.

$$(\hat{x}, \text{TILT}) * (\hat{y}, -\text{PAN}) * z_3 * y_3 * i * (\hat{z}, \text{SH\_ORI})$$
$$* i * y_3 * y_1 * y_1 * i * i * i * i \quad\quad (6.2)$$

When the five rules SR1,..., SR5 are applied, the much simpler expression

$$z_3 * (\hat{y}, \text{TILT}) * (\hat{x}, \text{PAN} - \text{SH\_ORI}) \quad\quad (6.3)$$

is obtained. (In this case SR3 had no effect.)

The appearance of a given object may be invariant with respect to certain changes in relative orientation of object and camera. The standard form for the rotation expressions was chosen to make it easy to further simplify the expression by making use of such invariants. Section 7.3.2 gives an example of this. The standard form for rotation expressions also happens to be very convenient for the simplification of the translational component of a coordinate transform.

6.3.2 Simplification of Translation Expressions

Simplification of translation expressions is quite straightforward, and relies on the rules given below. Rule SR6 is applicable to a product of rotations in the standard form described in the previous section. Rules SR7,..., SR11 are applicable to a sum of terms, each of which is a product of rotations applied to a vector.

SR6: Shift elementary z-axis rotations to the right end of products of rotations.

SR7: For each term in the sum, apply rule SR6 to the rotation product, then apply the elementary rotations at the right to the vector, by permuting its components and changing their signs appropriately.

SR8: Remove terms in the sum where the vector is zero.

SR9: Collect terms with symbolically identical rotation expressions, by symbolically summing the components of the vectors to which they are applied, then apply rule SR8.

SR10: In each term remove a right-most rotation from the rotation product if its axis vector is collinear with the vector to which the product is being applied.

SR11: While there is a term whose right-most rotation has an axis which is neither collinear with, nor normal to, the vector to which the product is applied, split the vector into collinear and normal component vectors, replace the single term with the two new ones formed in this way, and apply rule SR10.

In the process of determining the translation component of a transform expression by using equation (6.1) the geometric simplification system simplifies all the rotation products in the terms of the sum. To simplify the final translation expression, rules SR7, SR9, and SR11 are applied in order. The following is the expression for the position of the screwdriver *tool* in camera coordinates in the situation shown in the left of figure 6.1:

$$(\hat{x}, \text{TILT}) \otimes (0, -21.875, 0)$$
$$+ (\hat{x}, \text{TILT}) * (\hat{y}, \text{SH\_ORI} - \text{PAN}) \otimes (0, 0, 1) \qquad (6.4)$$
$$+ (\hat{x}, \text{TILT}) * (\hat{y}, -\text{PAN}) \otimes (\text{SH\_Y} - 30, 0, \text{SH\_X} - 83.5)$$

The original unsimplified form is far too large to warrant inclusion here. The simplified form is both tractable and useful as will be seen in chapter 7.

Finally note that it is simple to subtract one translation expression from another. In the translation to be subtracted, simply negate each component of the vector in each of its terms, symbolically add the two translations by appending the lists of terms, then simplify as above.

7

Prediction

Prediction is used to build the *prediction graph* which provides a prediction of observable features and their relations which should be matched by features in an image. Prediction has two other major uses however. The first is to provide direction to the low level descriptive processes. This is described in appendix A2. The second is to provide instructions on how to use image measurements to understand the three-dimensional aspects of the objects which gave rise to the measured image and thus to identify class memberships and specific three-dimensional spatial relationships. An interpretation algorithm (described in chap. 8) is used to hypothesize matches of observations to predictions, to apply the resulting constraints to models, and to combine local interpretations into globally consistent interpretations.

The ACRONYM predictor is implemented as a collection of some 280 production-like rules. The main control structure is backward chaining, although there is an agenda mechanism which is used occasionally for forward reasoning. The production rules are translated into MACLISP functions and translated into machine code. An overview of this process is given in appendix A3.

The preceding chapters have dealt with many of the specific mechanisms used for prediction. This chapter gives an overview of how these mechanisms fit together. The first section describes in detail the form of the prediction graph. Section 7.2 describes how the geometric reasoning capabilities of the previous chapter are used to compute the implications of objects being observed. Sections 7.3 and 7.4 describe how to use geometric reasoning to find invariant characterizations of observables, and in particular how to predict image shapes. Section 7.5 details the observable relations which ACRONYM predicts on the basis of its geometric reasoning.

7.1 Producing the Prediction Graph

The prediction graph consists of nodes and arcs. The nodes are either predictions of specific image features, or recursively complete prediction graphs of finer level features. In the current implementation only shapes are predicted. The arcs of the graph specify relations between the nodes. The node types for shape predictions are detailed in section 7.4 and the arc types for predictions of relations are detailed in section 7.5.

A prediction graph has associated with it a restriction node, which refers to the object class being predicted. It could also be the *base-restriction,* the most general restriction node, in which case the graph predicts the whole scene which appears in the image to be interpreted. Each graph node and arc has a restriction node associated with it also. Those associated with prediction nodes must be at least as restrictive as that associated with the graph itself. Those associated with prediction arcs must be at least as restrictive as those associated with the arc's two nodes.

7.1.1 Invariant and Quasi-Invariant Observables

The best things to predict about the appearance of an object are those which will always be observable. An *observable* is defined as something which can be observed in an image; it is either a feature which might be described directly by the low-level processes, or it is a directly computable relation between observables. Something is said to be an *invariant observable* if it is constant and observable over the whole range of variations in model size and structure, and its spatial relation to the camera coordinate system.

For instance, colinear straight line segments in three-space which are observable give rise to colinear straight line segments in images for all camera coordinates.

Sometimes the search for invariants will be unsuccessful. Often when there are no invariants directly available, ACRONYM is able to carry out case analysis. It produces new restriction nodes, descendents of the old, each with additional constraints, which restrict the situation in each restriction node to one where there are adequate invariants available. The additional constraints are chosen so that the lattice supremum of the new restriction nodes is the original node. The new restriction node is then associated with the prediction node or arc.

Sometimes case analysis is not enough. Expressions concerning orientations may be too complex for complete symbolic analysis. However it may be that some of the terms make no qualitative difference to predictions. This is often the case when quantifiers are sufficiently constrained that an expression is restricted to a small region about local maxima, minima, or points of inflexion. Expressions are hard to analyze symbolically in such regions. Often some prediction based on such an expression is nearly invariant over the modeled range of variations. Thus a reasonable prediction may be made by ignoring the difficult term in an expression. Where an invariant is found by ignoring a small effect of some term it is called a *quasi-invariant.* The most common instances of quasi-invariants arise from ignoring cosine terms with small arguments. The ACRONYM implementation of this idea takes into account the errors so produced. A quantitative analysis of the process is given below in section 7.3.3.

7.1.2 Shapes and Relations

In the current implementation of ACRONYM, prediction nodes predict shapes that will appear in the image. Prediction arcs are expected relations between such shapes.

To predict the shapes generated by a single generalized cone, or to predict the relations between shapes from different generalized cones, ACRONYM does not explicitly predict all possible qualitatively different viewpoints. That is, it does not attempt total prediction, only partial predictions. Predictions concern what shapes generated by visible surfaces might appear in the image and have associated with them methods to compute constraints on the model that are implied by their individual appearance in an image. For example, identification of the image of the swept surface of a right circular cone constrains the relative orientation of the cylinder to the camera (these are called back constraints—see sec. 7.4). Identification of an end face of the cylinder provides a different set of constraints. If both the swept surface and an end face are identified, then both sets of constraints apply. Specific relations are predicted between shapes that will be observable if both the shapes are observed correctly. For more complex cones, the payoff is even greater from predicting individual shapes rather than exhaustive analysis of which shapes can appear together.

At other times during prediction, invariant cases of obscuration are noticed. For instance it may be noticed that one cone abuts another so that its end face will never be visible. The consequences of such realizations are propagated through the predictions.

Prediction of shapes proceeds in five phases.

First, all the contours on a generalized cone which could give rise to image shapes are identified by a set of special purpose rules. These include occluding contours and contours due purely to internal cone faces. For instance, a right square cylinder will generate contours for the end faces, the swept faces, and contours generated by the swept edges at diagonally opposite vertices of the square cross section. The contours are generated independently of camera orientation and in terms of object dimensions rather than image quantities.

Second, the orientation of the generalized cone relative to the camera (this is done by the geometric reasoning system as described in sec. 7.3) is then examined to decide which contours will be visible and how their image shapes will be distorted over the range of variations in the model parameters that appear in the orientation expressions.

The third phase predicts relations between contours of a single generalized cone (see sec. 7.5).

Fourth, the actual shapes that the contours will generate are predicted. The expected values for shape parameters in the image are estimated as closed intervals (see sec. 7.4).

Fifth, the back constraints which will be instantiated during interpretation are constructed. These are also described in detail in section 7.4.

After shapes have been predicted for single generalized cones, the relations between shapes of separate generalized cones are predicted. The same mechanisms are used as in phase three above.

7.2 Deciding on Visibility

Given a spatial reasoning capability, one of the simplest questions which can be asked when predicting the appearance of an object is whether the object will be visible at all. If it is known in advance that an object will definitely not be visible then a lot of time can be saved by not searching for it in the image. There are two ways that an object may not be visible. First it may be outside the field of view; then, even if it is in the field of view it may be obscured by another object closer to the camera.

It is quite straightforward to use the geometric simplification algorithms described in section 6.3 and the constraint manipulation system of section 5.4 (or more generally any constraint which can meet requirements A1 and A2 of sec. 5.2) to answer questions of possible invisibility.

To determine whether an object is in the field of view it is necessary to know its coordinates (c_x, c_y, c_z) in the camera frame of reference, and the *focal ratio* r of the camera (see sec. 4.1). In general these can all be expressions involving quantifiers. The z coordinate c_z must be negative for the object to be in front of the camera. In that case the image coordinates of the object are $(rc_x/-c_z, rc_y/-c_z)$, using a standard camera projection. These two components can be bounded using algorithms INF and SUP of section 5.4. The bounds are then compared to the extreme visible image coordinates (–0.5 and 0.5 by convention in ACRONYM), and whatever deductions possible are made (one of "definitely invisible," "definitely in field of view," or "perhaps in field of view").

For example, the expression

$$83.5 \cos(-PAN) \sin(TILT) + SH\_Y \sin(TILT) \sin(-PAN)$$
$$-21.875 \cos(TILT) - 30 \sin(TILT) \sin(-PAN)$$
$$-SH\_X \cos(-PAN) \sin(TILT) - \cos(SH\_ORI - PAN) \sin(TILT)$$

is the y camera coordinate c_y of the origin of the coordinate frame of the screwdriver tool in the camera geometry in the left image of figure 6.1. The z

camera coordinate is of similar complexity. For a focal ratio r of 2.42, algorithms INF and SUP provide bounds of –2.658 and 3.326 respectively, for the y image coordinate of the screwdriver tool. Thus ACRONYM can deduce that the screwdriver tool may indeed be visible. For a different set of constraints on the position quantifiers (SH_X and SH_Y) it can be deduced that the screwdriver tool is invisible even though its position and orientation and the pan and tilt of the camera are all uncertain.

Similar techniques can be used to decide whether an object might occlude another, whether over the whole range of variations in their sizes, structures, and spatial relations, over some ranges, or never. In this case it is better to examine the translation between the origins of their coordinate frames. This can be calculated by symbolically differencing their coordinates in the camera frame and simplifying as in the previous section. Various heuristics (implemented as rules in ACRONYM's predictor) can then be used to decide about occlusion possibilities.

For example, consider the camera overhead geometry which gives rise to the illustration in the right of figure 6.1. The expression for the position of the screwdriver holder base minus the position of the screwdriver tool is

$$(\hat{x}, -\text{ROLL}) * (\hat{y}, -\text{PITCH}) \otimes (0, 0, -2.625)$$
$$+ (\hat{x}, -\text{ROLL}) * (\hat{y}, -\text{PITCH}) * (\hat{z}, \text{SH\_ORI}) \otimes (-1, 0, 0)$$

Expanding this out and applying algorithms INF and SUP gives bounds of – 1.679 and 1.679 on the x component, –1.746 and 1.746 on y, and –3.143 and – 1.932 on the z component. Thus ACRONYM can conclude that the screwdriver holder base is always further from the camera than the screwdriver tool. One heuristic rule concludes that since the x and y components are comparable in size to the z component, it is possible that the screwdriver tool will appear in front of the screwdriver holder base in images. Another rule, however, says that since the view of the tool that can be seen (see sec. 6.5 for the deduction of the view to be seen) is small compared to the view that will be seen of the holder base, it will not interfere significantly with observation of the latter. (Actually in this case it is also concluded that the screwdriver tool is occluded always by the screwdriver motor above it. Also other subparts of both the screwdriver holder and the screwdriver itself interfere more with observation of the screwdriver holder base.)

Before leaving the subject of visibility, consider the following. If an object is visible, then its image coordinates must be within the bounds of the visible part of the image plane. Thus the expressions for the image coordinates, as calculated above, can be bounded above and below by 0.5 and –0.5 respectively, and those constraints are merged into the constraint set of the restriction node associated with the appropriate prediction node. If the object is visible it must satisfy those constraints anyway. Having the constraints explicitly stated may help prune some incorrect hypotheses as will be seen in chapter 8. Thus the constraints added are those that must be satisfied if something in the image is indeed an instance of that which is predicted.

Note that if the decision procedure as described in chapter 5 were actually a complete decision procedure, then it would suffice to simply merge the constraints (described in the previous paragraph) with those of the model and then test the constraint set for satisfiability to decide whether the object could be visible. However, since the decision procedure used is only partial and can not always detect unsatisfiable sets of constraints, the less direct procedure described above must be used. Even with the new constraints merged into the constraint set, algorithms SUP and INF may not produce image coordinate bounds of 0.5 and –0.5. This is because the bound on the expressions must be reconstructed from the normal form of the constraints, rather than referring directly to the newly added constraints. As was seen in section 5.4, SUP and INF produce only upper and lower bounds on expressions, not suprema and infima. Furthermore to keep the number of symbols in the constraint set at a reasonable level, ACRONYM does not use the image coordinate expressions directly in the bounds, but rather uses simplified bounding expressions as demonstrated in section 5.4.4.

7.3 Observable Feature Prediction

The current implementation predicts shapes as image features. The choice is driven by two considerations. First, the low-level descriptive processes available produce shape descriptions. Second, two-dimensional shape can be a good invariant characterization of how a generalized cone will appear in an image.

7.3.1 Ribbons and Other Shapes

The current implementation of ACRONYM uses *ribbons* and *ellipses* as the image features which low level processes produce. Ribbons are two-dimensional specializations of generalized cones. A ribbon is a planar shape which can be described by three components. The *spine* is a planar curve. A line segment, the *cross section,* is held at a constant angle to the spine, and swept along it varying according to the *sweeping-rule.*

Ribbons are a good way of describing the images generated by generalized cones. The perspective transformation preserves the generalized translational invariance common to both generalized cones and ribbons. Consider a ribbon which corresponds to the image of the swept surface of a generalized cone. For straight spines, the projection of the cone spine into the image would closely correspond to the spine of the ribbon. Thus a good approximation of the observed angle between the spines of two generalized cones is the angle between the spines of the two ribbons in the image corresponding to their swept surfaces. A quantitative theory of these correspondences is not given here.

Ellipses are a good way of describing the shapes generated by the ends of generalized cones. The perspective projections of ends of cones with circular cross section are exactly ellipses.

There are two descriptive modules. The second module consists of two algorithms (see app. A2 for details): first an edge linking algorithm based on best-first search, and second an algorithm to fit ribbons and ellipses to sets of linked edges. The descriptive module returns a graph structure, the *observation graph*. The nodes are ribbon (ellipse) descriptions. The arcs are observed image relations between ribbons; currently only image connectivity is precomputed, and then only if there is plenty of free address space—in practice this means that they are rarely precomputed. Other arc types are computed as needed. The module produces ribbons which have straight spines and sweeping-rules which describe linear scalings. The module provides information regarding orientation and position of the spine in image coordinates for ribbons, and position, orientation, and length of major and minor axes for ellipses. Figure 2.3, chapter 3, shows the action of these algorithms on an image.

7.3.2 *Invariant Shapes*

The most important factor in predicting shape is the orientation of the object relative to the camera. It is therefore potentially interesting to consider under what variations in orientation of an object relative to the camera, does its perceived shape remain invariant. In fact such invariants are very useful for reducing the complexity of the expressions derived, using the methods described in section 6.3.1 for object orientations, to manageable levels where shape can be predicted directly.

Note first that for a generalized cone which is small compared to its distance from the camera, perspective effects are small. There may still be strong perspective effects between such objects however. (For instance, cones with parallel spines defining a plane which is not parallel to the image plane will still have a vanishing point.) In any case it is therefore true that in predicting the apparent shape of such generalized cones, the perspective projection can be approximated with a slightly simpler projection. ACRONYM carries out shape prediction using a *perspective-normal* projection. For a generalized cone whose closest point to the camera has z coordinate z', the projection of a point (x, y, z) in three space into the image plane of a camera with focal ratio r is $(rx/(-z'), ry/(-z'))$ instead of $(rx/(-z), ry/(-z))$. Intuitively, this can be thought of as a normal projection into a plane which is parallel to the image plane, intersects the generalized cone, and is the closest such plane to the camera, followed by a perspective projection of the image into the camera. It is also equivalent to a normal projection scaled according to the distance of the object from the camera. Examples of why this is useful are given below. The perspective-normal projection in ACRONYM is further simplified by using the z camera coordinate of the origin of the cone coordinate frame, rather than z' as defined above.

Consider again, the problem of simplifying orientation expressions, while keeping the implied shape invariant. The normal form described in section 6.3.1 was designed with such problems in mind. First note that a rotation about the z-axis at the left of a rotation product corresponds to a rotation in the image plane (recall the definition of camera geometry in sec. 4.1). The two-dimensional shape descriptions used are invariant with respect to orientation, so all shape prediction is unaffected by ignoring such rotations. Thus for instance, the expression (6.3) for the orientation of the screwdriver tool in the left illustration of figure 6.1, is equivalent to

$$(\hat{y}, \text{TILT}) * (\hat{x}, \text{PAN} - \text{SH\_ORI}) \qquad (7.1)$$

for the purpose of predicting the shape of the image of the screwdriver tool. In general the standard form for rotation expressions has all elementary z-axis rotations moved to the left—ready to be ignored.

The screwdriver tool is a cylinder, with its spine (an axis of radial symmetry) along the x-axis of its coordinate system. Thus the appearance of the tool is invariant with respect to a rotation about $\hat{x}$. The right rotation of expression (7.1) can thus be ignored for the purpose of shape prediction, leaving

$$(\hat{y}, \text{TILT}) \qquad (7.2)$$

to be analyzed. In physical terms this says that the camera tilt is the only variable in the case in the left of figure 6.1 that is important for shape prediction.

Expression (7.2) is simple enough that special case rules are applicable. One says that the cylinder will appear as a ribbon generated by its swept surface, and an ellipse generated by its initial cross section. Furthermore they will be connected in the image. (If the descriptive process which found ellipses were able to accurately determine their major axis then another useful rule could come into play. From expression (7.2) it would deduce that in the image the major axis of the ellipse will be normal to the spine of the ribbon.) Later in the prediction it is decided that the ellipse corresponding to the top of the screwdriver tool will actually be occluded (as described in sec. 6.2), but that need not concern us here.

The screwdriver modeled in figure 6.1 is actually a particular screwdriver with specific dimensions. To make this example more general, suppose that the screwdriver tool has variable size, with its length represented by the quantifier TOOL_LENGTH and its radius by TOOL_RADIUS. Using the perspective-normal projection approximation, the length to width ratio of the ribbon corresponding to the swept surface of the screwdriver tool can be predicted to be:

$$\frac{\text{TOOL\_LENGTH} \times \cos(\text{TILT})}{\text{TOOL\_RADIUS}}.$$

Consider the ellipse corresponding to the top of the screwdriver tool. The ratio of its minor axis to its major axis is simply:

$$\sin(\text{TILT}).$$

Thus the range of shapes that can be generated has been comprehensively predicted. The actual form in which these predictions is used is not just to establish a predicate against which hypothesized shape matches will be tested. They are used in a more powerful way, described in chapter 7, to actually extract three dimensional information about the viewed scene.

Besides shape, bounds on the dimensions of objects can also be predicted. This, too, is used to extract three-dimensional information as described in chapter 7. Size bounds have a more immediate application, however. They are used to direct the low-level descriptive processes [20] which search the image for candidate shapes to be matched to predictions. Given that the focal ratio is 2.42 and the length of the screwdriver tool is 1, and using the expanded z component of (6.4), the algebraically simplified prediction of the length of the ribbon in the image is:

$$-2.42 \cos(\text{TILT})/(30 \cos(\text{TILT}) \sin(-\text{PAN}) + \text{SH\_X} \times \cos(-\text{PAN})$$
$$+ \cos(\text{TILT}) \cos(\text{SH\_ORI} - \text{PAN}) - 21.875 \sin(\text{TILT})$$
$$- 83.5 \cos(\text{TILT}) \cos(-\text{PAN})$$
$$- \text{SH\_Y} \times \cos(\text{TILT}) \sin(-\text{PAN}))$$

Algorithms INF and SUP are used to determine that this quantity is bounded by 0.0190 and 0.0701, information which can be used by the descriptive processes to limit the search for candidate ribbons in the image. These are not particularly accurate estimates on the infimum and supremum of the above expression because it contains sines and cosines which have coupled arguments, but the constraint manipulation system treats them independently and makes the most pessimistic bounds. However they are still exceedingly useful for limiting search.

In general, at the right of the standard form for a product of rotations is one of six elementary rotations: i(implicitly only), y_1, y_3, x_1, and x_3. If there are not other rotations in the expression these correspond to the six views of a generalized cone from along the positive and negative coordinate axes. Rotations y_1 and y_3 correspond to viewing the initial and final cross-sections swept to form the generalized cone. The others correspond to four orthogonal views of the swept surface of the generalized cone. In expression (6.3) the right-most elementary rotation is implicitly the identity i, which corresponds to a side view of the cylinder. In trying to reduce the complexity of the orientation expression, ACRONYM essentially tries to find how the nonelementary rotations change the viewpoint from one of the six primitive viewpoints of a generalized cone.

As a final example consider the orientation expression derived for the screwdriver tool in the camera geometry illustrated in the right of figure 6.1:

$$(\hat{x}, - \text{ROLL}) * (\hat{y}, - \text{PITCH}) * (\hat{z}, \text{SH\_ORI}) * y_1$$

Here the right-most elementary rotation is y_1 which corresponds to viewing the initial cross section of the cylinder of the screwdriver tool. In the modeled situation that is the top of the cylinder, but that is not derivable from this expression with as simple an analysis as used in expression (6.3). Various heuristic rules try rearranging the expression to find a situation in which an invariant simplification can be detected. One such rule tries shifting the right-most elementary rotation left one position. Using the identities of section 6.3 this gives the expression:

$$(\hat{x}, - \text{ROLL}) * (\hat{y}, - \text{PITCH}) * y_1 * (\hat{x}, - \text{SH\_ORI})$$

As in the previous example there is an x-axis rotation at the right. A cylinder's appearance is invariant with respect to a rotation about its axis, so the simplified expression:

$$(\hat{x}, - \text{ROLL}) * (\hat{y}, - \text{PITCH}) * y_1 \tag{7.3}$$

can be used for predicting shape.

ACRONYM has special case rules which handle expressions such as (7.3) when there are at most two nonelementary rotations left in the expression.

7.3.3 Quasi-Invariants

Sometimes there may be no rule in ACRONYM's rule-base which is able to predict the shapes on the basis of the drived orientation expression. The problem is that there may be more than two rotations with uncertain magnitude.

However, if some of the rotations have small magnitude their effects on the perceived shape of the object depend roughly on the cosines of their magnitudes. If the cosines are almost constant over the modeled range of variations then for shape prediction at least they can be effectively ignored; the error involved in doing so will be smaller than the errors incurred by low-level descriptive processes. Heuristic rules, written on the basis of error analyses, are used to identify such cases. The effect of the errors so introduced are taken into account by determining the range of values that can be taken by the product of the cosines of the ignored angles. These bounds are factored into the forward predictions and the backward constraints, but no back constraints attempt to estimate the errors and bound the ignored angles.

The current rules in ACRONYM are willing to ignore rotations whose magnitudes are such that the product of their cosines is bounded by the interval [0.9, 1.0].

7.4 Forward and Backward Constraints

Algebraic constraints are used in two ways. Constraints given by the user to define model classes are used in a *forward* manner to make predictions of measurements which will be made in images. When an image feature or image feature relation is hypothesized to correspond to a prediction in the prediction graph, measurements may be made from the image data. These measurements are used to construct new algebraic constraints which are placed *back* on the original model. The new constraints specialize the model class down to the subclass which could possibly have given rise to the observed measurements.

Consider the problem of predicting the length of an image feature which is generated by something of length l, lying in a plane parallel to the camera image plane, at distance d from the camera. Furthermore suppose the camera has a focal ratio of f. Then the length of the image feature is given by $p = (l \times f)/d$. Any or all of l, f, and d may be expressions in quantifiers, rather than numbers. Using the CMS, bounds can be obtained on the prediction expression p giving that it will lie in some range $P = [p_l, p_h]$ where p_l and p_h are either numbers or $\pm\infty$. For more complex geometries the expression for p will be more complex, but the method is the same (trigonometric functions are usually involved—see the next section). This is an example of the *forward* use of constraints.

Later the interpreter may hypothesize that a certain image feature corresponds to the prediction. It has to decide whether it is acceptable on the basis of its parameters. The low level descriptive processes are noisy and provide an error interval, rather than an exact measurement for image parameters. Suppose the measurement is $M = [m_l, m_h]$ for a feature parameter predicted with expression p. Then the parameter is acceptable if $P \cap M$ is nonempty. This is the coarse filtering used during initial hypothesis of image feature to feature prediction matches.

But note also that it must be true that the true value of p for the particular instance of the model which is being imaged must lie in the range M. Thus the following constraints can be added

$$m_l \leq (l \times f)/d$$
$$m_h \geq (l \times f)/d$$

to the instance of the model being hypothesized, where l, f, and d are numbers or expressions in quantifiers. These are called *back* constraints.

7.4.1 Trigonometric Back Constraints

When the prediction expression p involves trigonometric functions, the above method of generating back constraints will not work. It would generate constraints involving trigonometric functions, which ACRONYM's CMS cannot handle.

One approach to this problem is to bound expression p above and below by expressions involving no quantifiers contained in arguments to trigonometric functions, and then use these expressions in setting up the back constraints. This has the unfortunate side effect of losing all information implied by the image feature about the quantifiers eliminated from the bounds.

A second approach is sometimes applicable. If a trigonometric function has as its argument e, an expression, and if the CMS determines that e is bounded to lie within a region of the function's domain where it is strictly monotonic and hence invertible, then specific back constraints on e can be computed at interpretation time (as distinct from during prediction). This is illustrated with an example. Consider the cylindrical tool in the left of figure 6.1. Recall that it has length TOOL_LENGTH. In section 7.3 it was shown that the orientation of the cylinder relative to the camera was given by the rotation

$$(\hat{y}, \text{TILT}).$$

The predictor decides that the tool will appear as a ribbon generated by the swept surface of the cylinder. It predicts that the length of the ribbon in the image will be:

$$\frac{-2.42 \times \text{TOOL\_LENGTH} \times \cos(\text{TILT})}{\text{TOOL.CAMZ}}$$

where 2.42 is the focal ratio of the camera and TOOL.CAMZ is an internal quantifier generated by the prediction module.

Both of the above approaches are used to generate back constraints to ensure coverage of all the relevant quantifiers. They are:

$$m_h \geq -2.09578145 \times \text{TOOL\_LENGTH} \times (1/\text{TOOL.CAMZ})$$
$$m_l \leq -2.33754054 \times \text{TOOL\_LENGTH} \times (1/\text{TOOL.CAMZ})$$
$$\text{TILT} \geq \arccos(\sup(-0.413223144 \times m_h \times \text{TOOL.CAMZ}$$
$$\times (1/\text{TOOL\_LENGTH})))$$
$$\text{TILT} \leq \arccos(\inf(-0.413223144 \times m_l \times \text{TOOL.CAMZ}$$
$$\times (1/\text{TOOL\_LENGTH})))$$

The first two are nontrigonometric back constraints and at interpretation time a simple substitution of the measured numeric quantities for m_l and m_h is done. The latter two require further computation at interpretation time. After the substitution, expressions must be bounded over the satisfying set of all the known constraints, and the function arccos applied to give numeric upper and lower bounds on the quantifier TILT.

The techniques described here work for a more general class of functions than trigonometric functions (in the current implementation of ACRONYM it is used for functions sin, cos, and arcsin). The requirement is that the domain of the function (e.g., the interval $[-\pi, \pi]$ for sin and cos), can be subdivided into a finite number of intervals over which the function is strictly monotonic and hence locally invertible.

Recall that there are special case rules in the predictor rule-base for the various possible orientation expressions. These rules predict shapes as ribbons or ellipses, and construct prediction expressions for their parameters. Other special case rules recognize the form of the prediction expressions and set up instructions for constructing the back constraints.

7.4.2 Multiple Back Constraints

The previous example dealt only with constraints derivable from hypothesizing a match with a single ribbon. In identifying instances of an object whose description is more complex than a single generalized cone, there will be more than one primitive shape feature matched. Each provides a number of such back constraints which combine to further constrain the individual parameters.

Suppose an object is modeled with a well-determined size, position, and orientation. When constraints from hypothesized matches for many objects are combined, that particular object will be extremely useful for determining parameters of the camera and other objects. If there are many such tightly constrained modeled objects, then they are even more useful. Thus a mobile robot can use known reference objects to visually determine its absolute location and orientation, and the absolute location and orientation of other movable objects.

In a bin-picking task the camera parameters and location of the bin are probably well determined (although ACRONYM would not be at a loss if this were not the case). The problem is to distinguish instances of an object and determine its orientation so that a manipulator can be commanded to pick it from the bin. There will be many instances of each predicted image feature as there will be many instances of each object. The back constraints provide a mechanism for the interpretation algorithm to find mutually consistent features, and thus identify object instances. Furthermore the back constraints provide information on the position and orientation of the object instance.

In aerial photographs the back constraints tend to relate scale factors to camera height and focal ratio. Thus a single identifiable landmark can provide one tight relationship between these parameters. Derived back constraints from other objects interact to give relatively tight bounds on all unknowns.

7.5 Observable Feature Relation Prediction

Image feature (shape) predictions are organized as the nodes of the *prediction graph*. The arcs of the graph predict image-domain relations between the features. During interpretation, pairs of hypothesized matches of image features to prediction nodes are coarsely checked for consistency by attempting to instantiate the prediction arcs. Some arcs also include back constraints which the instantiation of the arc implies about the model. These are treated in exactly the same manner as those associated with image feature predictions.

Prediction arcs are generated to relate multiple shapes predicted for a single cone. For instance a right circular cylinder prediction includes shapes for the swept surface and perhaps each of the end faces (depending on whether the camera geometry is known well enough to determine a priori exactly which faces will be visible). It can be predicted that a visible end face will be coincident with a visible swept surface at at least one point in the image. (In fact a stronger prediction can be made: the straight spine of the swept surface image ribbon can be extended through the center of mass of the elliptical image of the end face.)

Prediction arcs are also generated between shapes associated with predictions for different generalized cones. These are actually of more importance in arriving at a consistent global interpretation of collections of image features as complex objects.

As an example of the geometric reasoning necessary to predict feature relations, consider the case of colinearity mentioned earlier in this chapter. Colinearity arcs are typically generated to relate the spines of two ribbons generated by swept surfaces of two cones by determining that the generalized cones have colinear spines in three-space. In the model the spines of generalized cones lie along the x-axis of their local coordinate system. The relative orientations of these coordinate systems can be determined by inverting the orientation of one with respect to the camera (this simply involves reversing the order of the rotation product and inverting the sign of the rotation magnitudes) and multiplying on the right by the orientation of the other, and applying the simplification algorithm of section 6.3.1 followed by rule SR6 of section 6.3.2. This produces a rotation expression with the minimal number of symbols possible, and it contains at most one elementary rotation. If the resulting expression is a product of rotations containing only the elementary rotations i, y_2, z_2, and rotations of the form $(\hat{x}, a)$ for arbitrary expressions a, then the spines are certainly parallel, and perhaps colinear. To decide whether the spines are indeed colinear requires examination of the translation between their local coordinate systems. The camera coordinates of one can be subtracted from the other as described in section 6.3.2. If the y and z components of the resulting vector are zero, then the object features are colinear.

The semantics of the arc types currently used are as follows:

7.5.1 Exclusive

If a generalized cone has a straight spine, and during sweeping, the cross section is kept at a constant angle to the spine, then at most one of the cone's end faces can be visible in a single image. *Exclusive* arcs relate image features which are mutually exclusive for this or other reasons. (Note that in this case, instantiations of the two end faces would probably result in inconsistent back constraints being applied to the spatial orientation of the original model, so that eventually the CMS would detect an inconsistency. However checking for the existence of a simple arc at an early stage is computationally much cheaper than waiting to invoke the decision procedure.)

7.5.2 Colinear

If two straight line segments in three-space are *colinear* then any two-space image of them will either be a single degenerate point or two colinear line segments. As was pointed out earlier, the spine of the image shape corresponding to the swept surface of a cone is usually a good approximation to the projection of the spine of the cone into the image. Thus if two cones are known to have colinear spines in three dimensions, a colinear spine arc between the predictions of their swept surfaces can be included.

7.5.3 Coincident

If two cones are physically *coincident* at some point(s) in three-space, then for any camera geometry, if they are both visible then their projections will be coincident at some point(s) (except for some cases of obscuration). Failure to match predicted coincident arcs turns out to be the strongest pruning process during image interpretation.

7.5.4 Angle

If the *angle* between the spines of two generalized cones as viewed from the modeled camera is invariant over all the rotational variations in the model, or if an expression for the observed angle can be symbolically computed and is sufficiently simple, then a prediction of the observed angle can be made. For example wing—wing and wing-fuselage angles are invariant when an aircraft is viewed from above—this is because the only rotational freedom of an aircraft on the ground is about an axis parallel to the direction of view of an overhead camera. Again the fact that the projections of model spines correspond to image spines is used here. This arc type includes (trigonometric) back constraints which make use of the observed angle. Some such constraints constrain relative spatial orientations of generalized cones. Others provide constraints on the orientation of the plane of rotation, which generated the angle, relative to the camera, and hence constraints on an object's orientation relative to the camera.

7.5.5 Approach-Ratio

Suppose a cone B is affixed at one end of its spine to another cone A, with a straight spine, somewhere along its length. The spines need not be coincident, but the cones must be. (See fig. 7.1.) Suppose the spine of cone A has endpoints a_1 and A_2, and let a_3 be the point on the spine of A closest to the end of the spine of B. Then the *approach-ratio* is the ratio of the length of the spine segment from a_1 to a_3 and the length of the complete spine from a_1 to a_2. If the spines of A

Figure 7.1.   The approach-ratio relation is defined for cones *A* and
B. Here only their spines are shown.

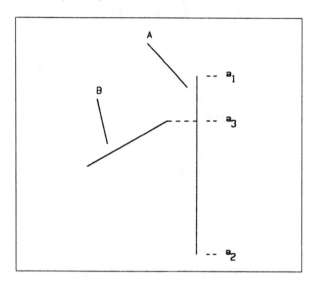

and *B* are both observable, then the approach-ratio is invariant under a normal projection for all camera geometries. Thus it is a quasi-invariant for a perspective projection for a camera sufficiently far from the object. For example, the ratio of the distance from the rear of the fuselage to the point of wing attachment, to the length of the fuselage, is almost invariant over all viewing angles for objects sufficiently far from the camera. Again this relies on the correspondences between the projection of a cone spine and the spine of the ribbon generated by the image of its swept surface. Approach-ratio arcs are only generated for pairs of image features which have a coincident arc. They provide back constraints on the model via the symbolic expression which describes the modeled spine projection ratio.

7.5.6 Distance

Sometimes symbolic expressions for the image distance between two image features can be computed. *Distance* arcs are only generated for pairs of image features which also have an angle arc, but no coincident arc. Distance arcs generate back constraints on the original model.

7.5.7 Ribbon-Contains

This is a directed arc type which two-dimensionally relates two predicted ribbons, one of which will contain the other in the image. For instance, *ribbon-*

contains arcs are built between the ribbon predicted from the occluding contour of a generalized cone with rectangular cross-section, and each of the ribbons generated by the two visible swept faces.

8

Interpretation

Interpretation proceeds by combining local matches of shapes to individual generalized cones, into more global matches for more complete objects (ACRONYM currently relies on shapes only). The global interpretations must be consistent in two respects. First, they must conform to the requirements specified by the arcs of the prediction graph. Second, the constraints that each local match implies on the three-dimensional model must be globally consistent; i.e., the total set of constraints must be satisfiable.

The interpreter is essentially a graph matcher. It tries to match maximal subgraphs of the *observation graph* to subgraphs of the *prediction graph*. Each such match is an *interpretation graph*. An interpretation graph consists of *interpretation nodes* and *interpretation arcs*. Each node (arc) is a unit with slots for a *prediction* and an *observation*. When an interpretation node (arc), is constructed these slots are filled by a prediction node (arc) and an observation node (arc) respectively. An interpretation node (arc) thus embodies a match between a prediction and an observation. Furthermore, the interpretation arcs must be consistent with the interpretation nodes in the sense that the prediction and observation nodes associated with the interpretation nodes joined by the arcs must be joined by the same prediction and observation arcs, respectively, which are associated with the interpretation arc.

Each interpretation node or arc has a restriction node associated with it. It is a specialization of the restriction associated with the prediction filling the prediction slot of the interpretation. It has all the back constraints added to it which are generated by hypothesizing the match (see sec. 7.4 for details of back constraints). Each complete interpretation graph has a restriction associated with it that is more restrictive than all those associated with its nodes and arcs. It may have extra constraints from matching variable numbers of subparts.

8.1 Local Matches

At a given time the interpreter looks for matches for a set of generalized cones, called the *search set*. They are cones determined by the predictor to have approximately equal importance in determining an interpretation for an image. Smaller generalized cones, corresponding to finer image features, are searched for later. Feature predictions include both an estimated range for feature parameters (e.g., ribbon length) and constraints on the model implied by hypothesizing a match with an image feature. The descriptive processes are invoked with direction from the first aspect of the predictions. The observation graph of features and observed relations between features is the result. Since the search set in general contains more than one generalized cone, not all the described features will match all, or even any, generalized cones in the search set. A comparison of all the image feature parameters with their range predictions is carried out to determine possible matches for each generalized cone in the search set (e.g., a ribbon's length and width must both fall in the predicted ranges to be considered further).

There is a question of partial matches for predicted features. The current descriptive processes used (see app. A2) partially take care of this problem in a fairly undirected manner. If edges associated with the two ends of a ribbon are observed by the line finder (Nevatia and Babu [46]), then the edge linking algorithm will probably hypothesize a ribbon, despite possible interference in the middle sections. (The strategy which works successfully is to make as many plausible hypotheses as possible at the lowest levels, so that the likelihood is low of missing a correct hypothesis which may be locally weak, and use the higher-level knowledge of the system to prune away the excess later.) Sometimes also, the predictor will predict specific obscurations and adjust its feature prediction accordingly. In general however, an additional mechanism which hypothesizes image features as partial matches for larger predictions may be very useful. Thus a ribbon might be hypothesized as being only one end of a larger ribbon, by not requiring that it fit the length prediction. It is also necessary in this case to increase the error estimate in the length measurement for the next stage of pruning, described below. ACRONYM does not currently include an implementation of these ideas.

The result of this first stage of matching and coarse pruning is a set of interpretation nodes whose prediction and observation slots are filled by matching prediction and observation nodes. A restriction node is built which is more restrictive than the restriction node which is associated with the prediction. It inherits the constraints from the prediction restriction, but also has added those back constraints built by following the instructions in the prediction. Often the new restriction node will be unsatisfiable and so the interpretation node can be eliminated from further consideration. For instance, both the length and width of a ribbon may fall in the predicted ranges, but perhaps the length is at the high end of the range, and the width at the low end. Then it is possible that the back constraints so generated will put inconsistent demands on the orientation of the object relative to the camera, or on some modeled constraint on the length to diameter ratio of the cone.

(For example in the generic class of jet aircraft, the fuselage lengths and diameters can vary greatly, but the length to diameter ratio varies much less. A constraint may be added to the model class expressing this fundamental relationship of overall scaling in aircraft.)

8.2 Propagating Arc Constraints

The interpreter tries to instantiate arcs of the prediction graph by pairwise checking hypothesized instantiations of predicted features which have a relation predicted between them. When there are multiple prediction arcs between two nodes, the instantiations are ordered by increasing cost of computing the observation arcs (recall that observation arcs are computed as needed). For instance, if a coincidence arc is predicted, that is checked first. If it can not be instantiated, then the remaining arcs can be ignored. Instantiation of arcs (other than *exclusive* arcs—see sec. 7.5.1) is similar to that of nodes. Gross predicted numeric ranges are checked first, then a restriction node is constructed which includes the constraints implied from image measurements of the relation. For instance, suppose an arc predicts a range of angles between the spines of two ribbons. First, the angle between the image spines must lie in the predicted numerical range. Then the back constraints associated with the arc may constrain the relation between the orientation of the object relative to the camera and the relative orientations in three space of the two generalized cones corresponding to the two ribbons.

A graph match is carried out to collect individual hypothesized instantiations of nodes and arcs into hypothesized connected components of interpretation graphs. The connectivity referred to here is that supplied by interpretation arcs which instantiate prediction arcs. *Exclusive* arcs prevent the collection together of some inherently mutually exclusive local interpretations. The algorithm used here is a variation on the constraint propagation algorithm introduced by Waltz [60] used for labeling line drawings.

In a previous implementation of the interpreter it was found that just pruning arc requirements was sufficient to carry out object classification correctly. In that implementation of the interpreter, only the simpler form of matching predictions to observations was used in which observation measurements were compared to prediction ranges, but no back constraining was done. The simple requirements specified by the arcs of the prediction graph, while only moderately strong by themselves, are very strong in conjunction with the requirements specified by the nodes. In experience with aerial images it was found to be extremely rare that two nodes and a connecting arc of the prediction graph were incorrectly instantiated in the observation graph. There was never encountered a case of a three-node, two-arc subgraph of the prediction graph being incorrectly instantiated.

The reasons for adding the constraint mechanism to a successful interpretation system are twofold. First, although the original scheme never incorrectly interpreted image features as an object instance, they sometimes failed to detect objects when predicted feature relations were not observed. Merely allowing subgraph matches, rather than complete graph embeddings, does lead to incorrect image interpretations. The constraint system allows for such relaxed matching, but still provides a mechanism for checking consistency of partial matches to separate connected components of the prediction graph. Second, the constraints provide a mechanism for gaining three-dimensional information from image interpretations.

8.3 Combining Back Constraints

As each connected component is built, interpretation restriction nodes are checked for consistency. The simplest way to do this would be to calculate the lattice infimum (actually use A3 of sec. 5.3), over the restriction nodes associated with the interpretations of each feature and feature relation. However in the general case, this can lead to some problems. For example, a class of aircraft may be modeled with the spines of generalized cones of the two wings each having their length slot filled with the quantifier WING_LENGTH. When combining local matches for the two wings of a single aircraft the constraints on WING_LENGTH should be consistent, as each wing should have the same length. However when combining two local interpretations of aircraft into, say, an interpretation of an image as an airfield, then the WING_LENGTH in the two cases refers to a different physical quantity. Individual aircraft have their wings the same length but different aircraft may have different wing lengths.

The term *conglomeration* is used to refer to the process of combining local interpretations, whether at the node and arc level, or when combining connected components of the interpretation graph. One result of conglomeration should be a new restriction node which is more restrictive than all the restriction nodes associated with the interpretations conglomerated. Of course it should be the least restrictive such restriction if possible.

Somehow the system has to decide whether quantifiers with the same name in two local matches refer to the same physical quantity. In an earlier paper [20] it was proposed that the user should include such information explicitly in the gometric models. However this information is actually implicitly available elsewhere and so a new scheme was developed, whereby the system decides itself from class rather than geometric considerations. As described in chapter 7, each prediction graph is associated with a particular user-supplied restriction node, which describes the class of objects predicted by the graph. In conglomerating submatches to the prediction graph, the system assumes that only quantifiers which are constrained in that restriction node refer to unique physical quantities. Therefore they are the only quantifiers retained in the conglomeration restriction node. For instance the restriction node describing the class of airfields does not mention WING_LENGTH, so constraints on that quantifier for each hypothesized aircraft on the airfield need not be mutually consistent.

The conglomeration restriction node is computed as follows. For each restriction node to be conglomerated, a more general restriction node containing only quantifiers to be retained is computed. For this purpose, algorithm INF is used on all upper bounds in the normal constraint form, and SUP on all lower bounds. In both cases the set H is the set of quantifiers to be retained, so all others are eliminated from the bounding expressions (see sec. 5.5.4). Then the lattice infimum of these new restriction nodes is calculated. If it is unsatisfiable, then the local interpretations associated with each of the restriction nodes are mutually inconsistent.

An alternative to eliminating quantifiers is to rename them, so that quantifiers referring to unique physical quantities have unique names. The advantage to this is that the current scheme of removing quantifiers leads to a weaker conglomeration restriction node which conceivably (but with very low probability) will allow an inconsistent interpretation to pass later in interpretation. By renaming quantifiers, no information is thrown away so no later errors can be introduced by the conglomeration process. The disadvantage is that the number of quantifiers and bounding expressions tends to grow (since all the common constraints have to be duplicated for the newly named quantifiers), making the higher levels of interpretation run roughly exponentially slower in the number of component interpretations. It seems that the advantages of renaming are small and the disadvantages great. Also by renaming variables, interpretation never proceeds to higher level abstractions, but is inherently always carrying around baggage from lower level details. For instance suppose the system has hypothesized a number of aircraft in an aerial view of an airfield, and then combines these in a global interpretation of an airfield instance. Without removing some variables from the conglomeration as is done in the current scheme it would be forced to carry around the variables for, say, the lengths of the engine pods of each aircraft. At best this is aesthetically unpleasing. Worse, the increasing complexity of constraint sets overwhelms the constraint manipulation system. In the current scheme, the individual interpretations for the aircraft contribute knowledge derived about the rest of the world from their local hypothesis, but then can be treated simply as atomic aircraft instances—a higher level abstraction.

8.4 Final Interpretations

At this stage the interpreter has hypothesized connected components of the interpretation graph. These may be complete components, in that they have instances of all predicted arcs and nodes, or they may only be partial (e.g., an interpretation may correspond to an aircraft except that no feature was found corresponding to the port wing). With each component is a restriction node which describes the constraints on the three-dimensional world implied by accepting that hypothesis. A combinatorial search is now carried out to find consistent connected components. Essentially this is done by deciding whether the restriction node produced as the conglomeration of the component restriction nodes is satisfiable. Conglomeration can also add constraints (equalities) on quantifiers used to describe variable numbers of subparts (e.g., the variable numbers of flanges on the electric motor in chap. 4). These constraints, too, of course, must be consistent with all the conglomerated restriction nodes.

Eventually, then, a number of interpretation graphs may be hypothesized. In general, some will be large and mostly correct interpretation graphs, and the others will be small, consisting of individual incorrect interpretations of parts of the image. The large graphs will be very similar in gross aspects, but may differ locally where they have accepted slightly different local interpretations. A single interpretation can be synthesized from the gross similarities. Experience shows that there are rarely competing interpretations of this nature.

A large correct interpretation graph has associated with it a restriction node which specializes both object models and their spatial relations to the three-dimensional understanding of the world derived from the feature prediction hypothesized matches in the interpretation graph. Other restriction nodes associated with components of the total interpretation may contain extra three-dimensional information pertinent to the appropriate local interpretation.

A final aspect of this scheme for interpretation is the ease with which subclass identification can be carried out once class identification has been achieved. Suppose there is an interpretation of a set of image features as an electric motor (see chap. 4 for the subclass definitions of this example). Associated with that interpretation is a restriction node. An immediate check can be made whether the interpretation is consistent with the object being an instance of some subclass of electric motors, e.g., *carbonator motor,* by taking the lattice infimum of the subclass restriction node and the interpretation restriction. If the infimum is unsatisfiable, then the object cannot be an instance of the subclass. If no inconsistency is found for several subclasses, but those subclasses themselves are inconsistent (i.e., the lattice infimum of their restriction nodes is known to be unsatisfiable), then perhaps prediction and search for finer features of the object must be carried out to resolve the classification.

9

Experimental Results

Along with detailed descriptions of the representations and algorithms used in ACRONYM, the previous chapters have shown various parts of the system at work on particular subproblems.

In this chapter the results of tying all the pieces together are demonstrated on some aerial images of airfield scenes. Models of some classes of aircraft and an aerial camera geometry are described to ACRONYM. It builds predictions from the models. Some preprocessed images are given to it, and it extracts shape descriptions. An interpretation of the image is made in terms of the original models.

A major limitation to experimentation with the ACRONYM system is the small address space available in the PDP-10 architecture. A great deal of effort has been expended in two directions to alleviate the problems that this causes ACRONYM. The first was to build a general multi-fork capability for use in the MACLISP environment. Then ACRONYM was partitioned into two forks (address spaces). A secondary fork contains just the low-level descriptive modules—PEMM. The primary fork contains all of ACRONYM that is necessary to carry out modeling, prediction, and interpretation. Other parts of ACRONYM are not loaded into this vision-version at all. This separation of ACRONYM into a vision-version, a simulation-version, etc., was the second part of the attempt to overcome address space limitations. Unfortunately there is still very little working space left in the primary fork, so that the garbage collector must constantly be at work and ACRONYM usually runs out of address space before completing an example. One solution would be to try to partition the primary fork again. However, coupling across forks is by way of files and so it is necessary that the modules in different forks are able to work efficiently with only occasional interactions with the other fork. Otherwise the system is slower in wall clock time by a few orders of magnitude. Since in the primary fork, the modeling system and the predictor share the object graph and the restriction graph, and the predictor and interpreter share the prediction graph and the restriction graph, it does not seem possible to find a satisfactory partition.

9.1 The Modeled Situation

In the examples to be described here, ACRONYM was given a generic model of wide-bodied passenger jet aircraft, along with class specializations to L-1011s and Boeing-747s. (See app. A1 for the complete specification exactly as input to ACRONYM.) The Boeing-747 class had further subclass specializations to Boeing-747B and Boeing-747SP. The subclasses do not completely partition their parent classes. The classes are described by sets of constraints on some 30 quantifiers. Figure 9.1 shows instances of the two major modeled classes of jet aircraft. These diagrams were drawn by ACRONYM from the models given it to carry out the image interpretations. The constraints for the generic class of wide-bodied jets are given in figure 9.2. Units are meters.

Figure 9.1.   Instances of class models of Boeing-747s and L-1011s.

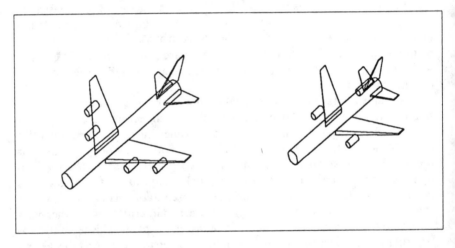

The camera was modeled as being between 1,000 and 12,000 meters above the ground. Thus there is little a priori knowledge of the scale of the images. A specific focal ratio was given: 20. (Similar interpretations have been carried out with a variable focal ratio, but then the final constraints on camera height and focal ratio are coupled, and not as clear for illustrative purposes— no accuracy is lost due to the nonlinearities that are introduced into the constraints, although both computation time and garbage collection time are increased.)

The aircraft models, the camera model, and the number of pixels in each dimension of the image (512 × 512 in these examples) were the only pieces of world knowledge input to ACRONYM. It has no special knowledge of aerial scenes: all its rules are about geometry and algebraic manipulation. These were applied to the particular generic models it was given, to make predictions and then to carry out interpretations.

Figure 9.2. Constraints on quantifiers in the generic model of wide-
bodied passenger jet aircraft.

```
ENG-DISP-GAP ε [6, 10]
ENG-DISP ε [0, 4]
ENG-GAP ε [7, 10]
STAB-ATTACH ε [3, 5]
R-ENG-ATTACHMENT ε [3, 5]
ENG-OUT ε [5, 12]
WING-ATTACHMENT ε [20, 40]
          WING-ATTACHMENT ≥ 0.4*FUSELAGE-LENGTH
          WING-ATTACHMENT ≤ 0.6*FUSELAGE-LENGTH
STAB-RATIO ε [0.2, 0.55]
STAB-SWEEP-BACK ε [3, 7]
STAB-LENGTH ε [7.6, 13]
STAB-THICK ε [0.7, 1.1]
STAB-WIDTH ε [5, 11]
RUDDER-RATIO ε [0.3, 0.4]
RUDDER-SWEEP-BACK ε [3, 9]
RUDDER-LENGTH ε [8.5, 14.2]
RUDDER-X-HEIGHT ε [7, 13]
RUDDER-X-WIDTH ε [0.7, 1.1]
WING-RATIO ε [0.35, 0.45]
WING-THICK ε [1.5, 2.5]
WING-WIDTH ε [7, 12]
          WING-WIDTH ≤ 0.5*WING-LENGTH
WING-LIFT ε [1, 2]
WING-SWEEP-BACK ε [13, 18]
WING-LENGTH ε [22, 33.5]
          WING-LENGTH ≥ 2*WING-WIDTH
          WING-LENGTH ≥ 0.43*FUSELAGE-LENGTH
          WING-LENGTH ≤ 0.65*FUSELAGE-LENGTH
REAR-ENGINE-LENGTH ε [6, 10]
ENGINE-LENGTH ε [4, 7]
ENGINE-RADIUS ε [1, 1.8]
FUSELAGE-RADIUS ε [2.5, 4]
FUSELAGE-LENGTH ε [40, 70]
          FUSELAGE-LENGTH ≥ 1.66666666*WING-ATTACHMENT
          FUSELAGE-LENGTH ≥ 1.53846154*WING-LENGTH
          FUSELAGE-LENGTH ≤ 2.5*WING-ATTACHMENT
          FUSELAGE-LENGTH ≤ 2.3255814*WING-LENGTH
R-ENG-QUANT ε [0, 1]
          R-ENG-QUANT ≤ 2 + -1*F-ENG-QUANT
F-ENG-QUANT ε [1, 2]
          F-ENG-QUANT ≤ 2 + -1*R-ENG-QUANT
```

9.2 The Descriptions

Figures 9.4 through 9.6 show three examples of interpretations carried out by
ACRONYM. In each case, part *a* is a halftone of the original grey-level image.
The *b* version is the result of applying the line finder of Nevatia and Babu[46].
That line finder was designed to find linear features such as roads and rivers in
aerial photos. Close examination of results on these images indicate many
errors and undue enlargement in width of narrow linear features. It also
produces many noise edges in smooth shading (not visible at the resolution of
the reproductions of these figures). These edges are the lowest level input to
ACRONYM.

An edge linker [20] is directed by the predictions to look for ribbons and ellipses. In this case there is very little a priori information about the scale of the images. The *c* versions of each figure show the ribbons fitted to the linked edges when it is searching for candidate matches for the fuselage and wings of aircraft. There is even further degradation of image information at this stage. This is the only data which the ACRONYM reasoning system is given to interpret. Notice that in the figure 9.6, almost all the shapes corresponding to aircraft are lost. Quite a few aircraft in 9.4 are lost also. Besides losing many shapes, the combination of the edge finder and edge linker conspire to give very inaccurate image measurements. All image measurements are assumed to have a ±30% error, except that for very small measurements, it is assumed that pixel noise swamps even those error estimates. Then the error is estimated to be inversely proportional to the measurement with a 2-pixel measurement admitting a 100% error. Thus the data which ACRONYM really gets to work with is considerably more fuzzy than indicated by the *c* series of figures.

It is planned to make use of new and better low-level descriptive processes being developed at Standford by other researchers as soon as they become robust enough for every day use (e.g., Baker [6] whose descriptions from stereo will also include surface and depth information).

9.3 The Interpretation

Despite the very noisy descriptive data, ACRONYM makes good interpretations of the images. The *d* series of figures show its interpretations with the ribbons labeled by what part of the model they were matched to. (The numbers which may be unreadable in 9.4*d* show the groupings into individual aircraft.)

ACRONYM first uses the most general set of constraints, those associated with the generic class of wide-bodied jets, when carrying out initial prediction and interpretation. Interpretation adds additional constraints for each hypothesized aircraft instance. For example in finding the correspondences in figure 9.5*d*, constraints were added which eventually constrained the WING_WIDTH (the width of the wings where they attach to fuselage) to lie in the range [7, 10.5677531] compared to the modeled bounds of [7, 12]. The height of the camera, modeled to lie in the range [1000, 12000] is constrained by the interpretation to the range [2199, 3322]. Figure 9.3 gives the full details of the constraints so added.

Once a consistent match or partial match to a geometric model has been found in the context of some set of constraints (model class), it easy to check whether it might also be an instance of a subclass. It is only necessary to add the extra constraints associated with the subclass and check for consistency with those constraints already implied by the interpretation using the CMS as described in chapter 8. The aircraft located in 9.5*d* is consistent with the constraints for an L-1011, but not for a Boeing-747. The author had examined the images previously and concluded that the aircraft was an L-1011. The additional symbolic constraints implied by accepting that the aircraft is in fact an L-1011 propagate through the entire constraint set. Although the constraints describing an L-1011 do not include constraints on camera height, the back constraints deduced during interpretation relate quantifiers representing such quantities as length of the wings to the height (and focal ratio in the more general case). Thus the height of the camera is further constrained in 9.5d to lie in the range [2356, 2489]. Recall that all image measurements were subject to ±30% errors, and that this estimate has taken all such errors into account. It may seem strange that a 5% error is derived from data with 30% errors. But consider the following simple case. Consider locating a point *(x, y)* in the square [0, 1] × [0, 1]. If *x* and *y* are specified with 10% error each, then the area of error for *(x, y)* is only 1%. This is similar to, but less complex than, what has happened in this interpretation.

Figure 9.4d indicates matches were found for three airplanes. Examination of the data in 9.4c indicates that this is the best that could be expected. Note however that only partial matches were found in all three cases. For such small ribbons, errors were apparently larger than the generous estimate used. The fuselage ribbon in the left-most aircraft (number 1) for instance fails to pass the coarse filtering stage. Despite the partial match, this particular aircraft is found to be consistent with the constraints for an L-1011, but not consistent with those of a Boeing-747. Again this is correct.

The other two aircraft identified are even more interesting. The author had thought from casual inspection of the grey-level image that they were instances of Boeing-747s. They both gave matches consistent with the class of wide-bodied jets. As expected, neither was consistent with the extra constraints of an L-1011. However, although each individual parameter range from the interpretation constraint sets was consistent with the individual parameter value or range for the class of Boeing-747s, neither set of constraints was consistent with that subclass (the constraints contain much finer information than just the parameter ranges—in the same way as in the example above where constraints on wing length propagate to constrain the camera height). On close examination of the grey-level image it was determined that the aircraft were not in fact Boeing-747's. The author used the fact that they were much smaller than the L-1011 to make that deduction, but the system made the deduction at the local level of shape before considering comparisons between aircraft.

The aircraft (probably Boeing-707s, but at the time of writing we have not yet obtained engineering drawings needed to build an accurate model for Acronym to check against the images) are in fact too small to be widebodied jets of any type. Since the scale of the image is unknown a priori this cannot be deduced locally. However it is reflected in the height estimates derived at the local level—[5400, 8226] interpreting the L-1011 just as a generic wide-body,

Figure 9.3.   Constraints on quantifiers after interpretation of figure 9.5a.

```
STARBOARD-WING.CAMZ ε [-3323.658, -2201.566]
        STARBOARD-WING.CAMZ ≥ -584.08894*WING-WIDTH
        STARBOARD-WING.CAMZ ≥ -99.213672*WING-LENGTH
        STARBOARD-WING.CAMZ ≥ -2.666668 + -1*HEIGHT
        STARBOARD-WING.CAMZ ≤ -314.50943*WING-WIDTH
        STARBOARD-WING.CAMZ ≤ -63.4227467*WING-LENGTH
        STARBOARD-WING.CAMZ ≤ -1.6666675 + -1*HEIGHT
STARBOARD-WING.CAMY ε [-∞, ∞]
        STARBOARD-WING.CAMY ≥ -44 + AIRCRAFT-Y
        STARBOARD-WING.CAMY ≤ 44 + AIRCRAFT-Y
STARBOARD-WING.CAMX ε [-∞, ∞]
        STARBOARD-WING.CAMX ≥ -44 + AIRCRAFT-X
        STARBOARD-WING.CAMX ≤ 44 + AIRCRAFT-X
AIRCRAFT-Y ε [-∞, ∞]
        AIRCRAFT-Y ≥ -44 + STARBOARD-WING.CAMY
        AIRCRAFT-Y ≥ -44 + PORT-WING.CAMY
        AIRCRAFT-Y ≤ 44 + STARBOARD-WING.CAMY
        AIRCRAFT-Y ≤ 44 + PORT-WING.CAMY
AIRCRAFT-X ε [-∞, ∞]
        AIRCRAFT-X ≥ -44 + STARBOARD-WING.CAMX
        AIRCRAFT-X ≥ -44 + PORT-WING.CAMX
        AIRCRAFT-X ≤ 44 + STARBOARD-WING.CAMX
        AIRCRAFT-X ≤ 44 + PORT-WING.CAMX
F-ENG-QUANT ε [1, 2]
        F-ENG-QUANT ≤ 2 + -1*R-ENG-QUANT
R-ENG-QUANT ε [0, 1]
        R-ENG-QUANT ≤ 2 + -1*F-ENG-QUANT
FUSELAGE-LENGTH ε [40.7801766, 70]
        FUSELAGE-LENGTH ≥ 0.0162526593*HEIGHT
        FUSELAGE-LENGTH ≥ 1.53846154*WING-LENGTH
        FUSELAGE-LENGTH ≥ 2.03900883*WING-ATTACHMENT
        FUSELAGE-LENGTH ≤ 0.0301835102*HEIGHT
        FUSELAGE-LENGTH ≤ 2.3255814*WING-LENGTH
        FUSELAGE-LENGTH ≤ 2.5*WING-ATTACHMENT
FUSELAGE-RADIUS ε [2.5, 4]
        FUSELAGE-RADIUS ≥ -1.05197865E-3*PORT-WING.CAMZ
        FUSELAGE-RADIUS ≥ 1.11117898E-3*HEIGHT
        FUSELAGE-RADIUS ≤ -1.75329772E-3*PORT-WING.CAMZ
        FUSELAGE-RADIUS ≤ 2.0636181E-3*HEIGHT
ENGINE-RADIUS ε [1, 1.8]
ENGINE-LENGTH ε [4, 7]
REAR-ENGINE-LENGTH ε [6, 10]
WING-LENGTH ε [22.6713915, 33.5]
        WING-LENGTH ≥ 1.7439532*WING-SWEEP-BACK
        WING-LENGTH ≥ -9.6637516E-3*PORT-WING.CAMZ
        WING-LENGTH ≥ -0.010079256*STARBOARD-WING.CAMZ
        WING-LENGTH ≥ 0.43*FUSELAGE-LENGTH
        WING-LENGTH ≥ 2*WING-WIDTH
        WING-LENGTH ≤ 2.12219682*WING-SWEEP-BACK
        WING-LENGTH ≤ -0.017946967*PORT-WING.CAMZ
        WING-LENGTH ≤ -0.0187186182*STARBOARD-WING.CAMZ
        WING-LENGTH ≤ 0.65*FUSELAGE-LENGTH
WING-SWEEP-BACK ε [13, 18]
        WING-SWEEP-BACK ≥ 0.471209828*WING-LENGTH
        WING-SWEEP-BACK ≤ 0.573409885*WING-LENGTH
WING-LIFT ε [1, 2]
```

Figure 9.3.　Continued.

```
WING-WIDTH ε [7, 10.5677531]
        WING-WIDTH ≥ -2.73539883E-3*PORT-WING.CAMZ
        WING-WIDTH ≥ -1.71206802E-3*STARBOARD-WING.CAMZ
        WING-WIDTH ≤ -5.0800263E-3*PORT-WING.CAMZ
        WING-WIDTH ≤ -3.1795549E-3*STARBOARD-WING.CAMZ
        WING-WIDTH ≤ 0.5*WING-LENGTH
WING-THICK ε [1.5, 2.5]
WING-RATIO ε [0.35, 0.45]
RUDDER-X-WIDTH ε [0.7, 1.1]
RUDDER-X-HEIGHT ε [7, 13]
RUDDER-LENGTH ε [8.5, 14.2]
RUDDER-SWEEP-BACK ε [3, 9]
RUDDER-RATIO ε [0.3, 0.4]
STAB-WIDTH ε [5, 11]
STAB-THICK ε [0.7, 1.1]
STAB-LENGTH ε [7.6, 13]
STAB-SWEEP-BACK ε [3, 7]
STAB-RATIO ε [0.2, 0.55]
WING-ATTACHMENT ε [20, 34.330405]
        WING-ATTACHMENT ≥ 0.4*FUSELAGE-LENGTH
        WING-ATTACHMENT ≤ 0.490434363*FUSELAGE-LENGTH
ENG-OUT ε [5, 12]
R-ENG-ATTACHMENT ε [3, 5]
STAB-ATTACH ε [3, 5]
ENG-GAP ε [7, 10]
ENG-DISP ε [0, 4]
ENG-DISP-GAP ε [6, 10]
HEIGHT ε [2198.89935, 3321.99133]
        HEIGHT ≥ 484.585785*FUSELAGE-RADIUS
        HEIGHT ≥ 33.130673*FUSELAGE-LENGTH
        HEIGHT ≥ -2.666668 + -1*STARBOARD-WING.CAMZ
        HEIGHT ≥ -2.666668 + -1*PORT-WING.CAMZ
        HEIGHT ≤ 899.94503*FUSELAGE-RADIUS
        HEIGHT ≤ 61.528393*FUSELAGE-LENGTH
        HEIGHT ≤ -1.6666675 + -1*STARBOARD-WING.CAMZ
        HEIGHT ≤ -1.6666675 + -1*PORT-WING.CAMZ
PORT-WING.CAMZ ε [-3324.658, -2200.566]
        PORT-WING.CAMZ ≥ -950.58964*FUSELAGE-RADIUS
        PORT-WING.CAMZ ≥ -365.577404*WING-WIDTH
        PORT-WING.CAMZ ≥ -103.479481*WING-LENGTH
        PORT-WING.CAMZ ≥ -2.666668 + -1*HEIGHT
        PORT-WING.CAMZ ≤ -570.35379*FUSELAGE-RADIUS
        PORT-WING.CAMZ ≤ -196.849373*WING-WIDTH
        PORT-WING.CAMZ ≤ -55.719722*WING-LENGTH
        PORT-WING.CAMZ ≤ -1.6666675 + -1*HEIGHT
PORT-WING.CAMY ε [-∞, ∞]
        PORT-WING.CAMY ≥ -44 + AIRCRAFT-Y
        PORT-WING.CAMY ≤ 44 + AIRCRAFT-Y
PORT-WING.CAMX ε [-∞, ∞]
        PORT-WING.CAMX ≥ -44 + AIRCRAFT-X
        PORT-WING.CAMX ≤ 44 + AIRCRAFT-X
```

Figure 9.4*a*. Interpretation by ACRONYM—gray level image.

Figure 9.4*b*. Application of line finder [46].

Figure 9.4*c*. Ribbons fitted to linked edges.

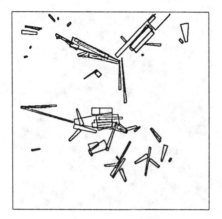

Figure 9.4*d*. ACRONYM's interpretation.

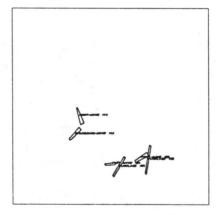

Figure 9.5a. Interpretation by ACRONYM—gray level image.

Figure 9.5b. Application of line finder [46].

Figure 9.5c. Ribbons fitted to linked edges.

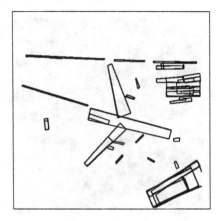

Figure 9.5d. ACRONYM's interpretation.

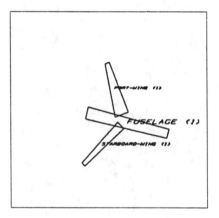

Figure 9.6*a*. Interpretation by ACRONYM—gray level image.

Figure 9.6*b*. Application of line finder [46].

Figure 9.6c. Ribbons fitted to linked edges.

Figure 9.6d. ACRONYM's interpretation.

([5786, 6170] as an L-1011), and [9007, 11846] for the right-most aircraft. Thus ACRONYM deduces that either the left aircraft is a wide-body and the others are not, or the right two are wide-bodies and the left one is not (it is too big).

Finally note that geometrically there were other candidates for aircraft in the ribbons of figure 9.4c. For instance the wing of the aircraft just to the right of those identified and a ribbon found for its passenger ramp could be the two wings of an aircraft with a fuselage missing between them. In fact these two ribbons were instantiated as an aircraft on the basis of the coarse filters on the nodes and arcs. However the set of back constraints they generated were mutually inconsistent.

Thus it can be seen from the examples that even with very poor and noisy data, the combined use of geometry and symbolic algebraic constraints can lead to accurate image interpretations. The system should be tested on more accurate low-level data to fully evaluate the power of this approach.

10

Implications

This study has concentrated on the predictive aspects of vision. The same is true of ACRONYM as a whole. That is not to say that descriptive processes are not vitally important for robust and accurate vision. Rather, the study has investigated the question of how to use models independently of particular descriptive processes that may eventually be available.

The study demonstrates that many of the requirements for the modeling and spatial understanding system are exactly those needed in other areas of motor-sensory functions. The same models and geometric reasoning capabilities are extremely useful for robot mobility and manipulation. Techniques were derived to deduce automatically three-dimensional information from descriptions of monocular images, in a general way.

The particular class representation given in chapter 4 is not universal. The remaining chapters, however, show how to use classes of models for understanding images. A more general representation of classes, e.g., inclusion of disjunctions in constraints, would require an upgrade of the various computing engines described (e.g., the constraint manipulation system and the geometric reasoning system). However, the interaction of these parts of the system could still operate in much the same manner.

Finally notice that there is no notion of assigning probabilities to local or global interpretations, nor is there any explicit underlying statistical model. While it is impossible to build a system with no inbuilt biases, an attempt has been made in ACRONYM to avoid such biases wherever possible. Any such biases are restricted to areas of geometric reasoning and are independent of the particular application domain. ACRONYM only "labels" parts of an image for which it can find a globally consistent interpretation.

Appendix 1

Example Model Specifications

Many models were used throughout the text of the thesis. Here we give the full input text to ACRONYM necessary to describe some of those models. The input language is fairly easy to understand without knowledge of the details of the syntax and semantics. Commentaries scattered throughout explain obscure points.

The input language is LISP-based and consists of a series of s-expressions. In general, order is not important (except in applying constraints) as forward references to undefined units always contain enough information to deduce the class of the unit, so a default is constructed, and it has its slots filled in later when an s-expression defining it is encountered. The character ";" is used for comments. It tells the LISP reader to ignore the rest of the input line.

The symbols "+:", "-:", "•:" and "%:" mean plus, minus, times and quotient respectively.

For clarity, all quantifiers and user-supplied unit names are typed in upper case and other symbols in lower case. This is only for the benefit of human readers and case is not taken into account by ACRONYM.

1.1 Library.

The following are taken from a small but growing library of prototype units, and user constants useful in most modeling applications. Succeeding sections of this appendix make frequent reference to them. A short commentary follows.

```
;;; unit vector constants

(user-constant XHAT (vector 1.0 0.0 0.0) T)
(user-constant YHAT (vector 0.0 1.0 0.0) T)
(user-constant ZHAT (vector 0.0 0.0 1.0) T)

;;; useful rotation magnitudes

(user-constant π π T)
(user-constant π%2 (*: π 0.5) T)
(user-constant 3π%2 (*: π 1.5) T)
(user-constant 2π (*: π 2.0) T)
(user-constant -π (-: π) T)
(user-constant -π%2 (*: π -0.5) T)
(user-constant -3π%2 (*: π -1.5) T)

;;; killable rotation magnitudes

(user-constant pi π)
(user-constant ZERO 0)

;;; standard sweeping rule

(define sweeping-rule CSW having type constant)
```

The function "user-constant" defines symbols (their first argument) as constants, but keeps their symbolic definition (second argument) around unevaluated so that editors such as MODITOR can show it to the user. The third argument is optional. If it is absent or null the algebraic simplifier will susbstitute the constant's value whenever it is encountered. If not null then the simplifier treats the symbol as a variable.

The final s–expression above defines a unit "CSW" as a sweeping rule which keeps cross–sections constant as they are swept along a spine.

1.2 Models of Wide–Bodied Jets.

Chapter 9 reported on some experimental results interpreting aerial images of airport scenes. For those experiments ACRONYM was given a generic model of wide-bodied passenger jet aircraft. This section contains the precise description input to ACRONYM. It has annotations interspersed in the same font as this.

The following statements declare the quantifiers which will be used in the model. The optional second argument to the function user-variable provides a default value to be used by the graphics module, in case it is asked to specify a model in the context of a restriction which does not completely specify the value of some quantifier.

```
;;; all the quantifiers

;;; structural quantifiers for engine configuration

(user-variable F-ENG-QUANT 1)
(user-variable R-ENG-QUANT 1)

;;; size quantifiers

(user-variable FUSELAGE-LENGTH 52.8)
(user-variable FUSELAGE-RADIUS 3.0)
(user-variable ENGINE-RADIUS 1.4)
(user-variable ENGINE-LENGTH 5.3)
(user-variable REAR-ENGINE-LENGTH 8.0)
(user-variable WING-LENGTH 25.1)
(user-variable WING-SWEEP-BACK 14.3)
(user-variable WING-LIFT 1.0)
(user-variable WING-WIDTH 7.5)
(user-variable WING-THICK 2.0)
(user-variable WING-RATIO 0.3333333)
(user-variable RUDDER-X-WIDTH 0.8)
(user-variable RUDDER-X-HEIGHT 8.3)
(user-variable RUDDER-LENGTH 10.3)
(user-variable RUDDER-SWEEP-BACK 4.8)
(user-variable RUDDER-RATIO 0.31)
(user-variable STAB-WIDTH 6.4)
(user-variable STAB-THICK 0.8)
(user-variable STAB-SPAN 9.5)
(user-variable STAB-SWEEP-BACK 4.0)
(user-variable STAB-RATIO 0.5)


;;; quantifiers used for purely for affixments

(user-variable WING-ATTACHMENT 24.0)
(user-variable ENG-OUT 7.6)
(user-variable ENG-GAP 0.0)
(user-variable ENG-DISP 0.3)
(user-variable ENG-DISP-GAP 0.0)
(user-variable R-ENG-ATTACHMENT 4.0)
(user-variable STAB-ATTACH 3.2)

;;; iteration variable

(user-variable I 1)
```

The following code defines the subpart tree and attaches the names of generalized cone descriptors to objects which have them. The function "spq" defines a unit which describes a quantified number of subparts of the same geometric class. Its first argument is an expression over quantifiers specifying the number of subparts. The second argument is the dummy word "of" and the third is the name of the geometric object class.

```
;;; subpart tree

(define object JET-AIRCRAFT having
   subpart FUSELAGE
   subpart PORT-WING
   subpart STARBOARD-WING)

(define object FUSELAGE having cone-descriptor FCONE
   subpart PORT-STABILIZER
   subpart STARBOARD-STABILIZER
   subpart RUDDER)

(define object PORT-WING having cone-descriptor PWC
   subpart (spq F-ENG-QUANT of PORT-ENGINE))

(define object STARBOARD-WING having cone-descriptor SWC
   subpart (spq F-ENG-QUANT of STARBOARD-ENGINE))

(define object PORT-ENGINE having cone-descriptor PEC)

(define object STARBOARD-ENGINE just-like PORT-ENGINE)

(define object RUDDER having cone-descriptor RDC
   subpart (spq R-ENG-QUANT of REAR-ENGINE))

(define object REAR-ENGINE having cone-descriptor REC)

(define object PORT-STABILIZER having cone-descriptor PSC)

(define object STARBOARD-STABILIZER having cone-descriptor SSC)
```

Next the affixment tree is defined. A coordinate transform between two objects is defined in terms of a translation vector of three components, each an expression over quantifiers and numbers, and a rotation. A rotation has an axis vector and a magnitude. In these examples the axes are all constant unit vectors from the library defined in the previous section. Notice that to affix engines to wings, simple affixment does not suffice as there is an unknown number of engines. The form "affix-iterate" is used. It affixes objects via a parameterized coordinate transform. ACRONYM can not represent affixments of variable numbers of objects with coordinate transforms which are not parameterizable in a single variable. The parameter is preceeded by the dummy word "over" and ranges over the integers from 1 up to the expression preceeded by the dummy word "upto".

```
;;; affixment tree

(affix FUSELAGE to JET-AIRCRAFT)

(affix PORT-WING to FUSELAGE with
        pos WING-ATTACHMENT FUSELAGE-RADIUS (*: -0.666667 FUSELAGE-RADIUS)
        ori π%2 about ZHAT)

(affix STARBOARD-WING to FUSELAGE with
        pos WING-ATTACHMENT (-: FUSELAGE-RADIUS) (*: -0.666667 FUSELAGE-RADIUS)
        ori -π%2 about ZHAT)

(affix-iterate PORT-ENGINE to PORT-WING
                with pos (+: ENG-OUT (*: (-: I 1) ENG-GAP))
                         (+: ENG-DISP (*: (-: I 1) ENG-DISP-GAP))
                         -1
                    ori -π%2 about ZHAT
                over I
                upto F-ENG-QUANT)

(affix-iterate STARBOARD-ENGINE to STARBOARD-WING
                with pos (+: ENG-OUT (*: (-: I 1) ENG-GAP))
                         (-: (+: ENG-DISP (*: (-: I 1) ENG-DISP-GAP)))
                         -1
                    ori π%2 about ZHAT
                over I
                upto F-ENG-QUANT)

(affix-iterate REAR-ENGINE to FUSELAGE
                with pos R-ENG-ATTACHMENT
                         0.0
                         (+: FUSELAGE-RADIUS ENGINE-RADIUS)
                over I
                upto R-ENG-QUANT)

(affix RUDDER to FUSELAGE with
        pos STAB-ATTACH 0 FUSELAGE-RADIUS
        ori -π%2 about YHAT)

(affix PORT-STABILIZER to FUSELAGE with
        pos STAB-ATTACH (*: 0.666667 FUSELAGE-RADIUS) 0.0
        ori π%2 about ZHAT)

(affix STARBOARD-STABILIZER to FUSELAGE with
        pos STAB-ATTACH (*: -0.666667 FUSELAGE-RADIUS) 0.0
        ori -π%2 about ZHAT)
```

In the code above that specified the subpart tree, forward references were also made to cone description units. They are defined here. They are slightly more complex than described in the body of the thesis; the complexity (use of "main-cone" and "simple-cone") is a remnant of an earlier design for ACRONYM. The necessary recoding to remove all traces of that design has not been carried out.

The definitions of the cones should be obvious, except perhaps for "non-perp" spines. These are straight lines running from the origin to the point

$$\left(\sqrt{\text{length}^2 - \text{y-disp}^2 - \text{z-disp}^2},\ \text{y-disp},\ \text{z-disp}\right).$$

Recall that the cross section lies in a plane parallel to the y–z plane.

Note that a "just-like" clause is sometimes used, to define a new unit using an old one as a prototype. It copies all the slot fillers of the old one, but some may be replaced by fillers in succeeding code.

```
;;; generalized cone descriptions

;;; cone descriptor for FUSELAGE

(define cone FCONE having
    main-cone (define simple-cone having
        cross-section (define cross-section having type circle
                                            radius FUSELAGE-RADIUS)
        spine (define spine having type straight length FUSELAGE-LENGTH)
        sweeping-rule CSW))


;;; cone descriptor for REAR-ENGINE

(define cone REC having
    main-cone (define simple-cone having
        cross-section (define cross-section having type circle
                                            radius ENGINE-RADIUS)
        spine (define spine having type straight length REAR-ENGINE-LENGTH)
        sweeping-rule CSW)))


;;; cone descriptor for RUDDER

(define cone RDC having
    main-cone (define simple-cone having
        cross-section (define cross-section having
                            type rectangle
                            width RUDDER-X-WIDTH
                            height RUDDER-X-HEIGHT)
        spine (define spine having
                            type non-perp
                            length RUDDER-LENGTH
                            y-disp 0.0
                            z-disp RUDDER-SWEEP-BACK)
        sweeping-rule (define sweeping-rule having type linear
```

```
                                            ratio RUDDER-RATIO)))


;;; cone descriptor for PORT-STABILIZER

(define cone PSC having
    main-cone (define simple-cone STAB having
       cross-section (define cross-section having
                                 type rectangle
                                 height STAB-THICK
                                 width STAB-WIDTH)
          spine (define spine AB having
                    type non-perp
                    length STAB-LENGTH
                    y-disp STAB-SWEEP-BACK
                    z-disp 0.0)
          sweeping-rule (define sweeping-rule having type linear
                                                 ratio STAB-RATIO)))


;;; cone descriptor for STARBOARD-STABILIZER

(define cone SSC having
    main-cone (define simple-cone just-like STAB having
       spine (define spine just-like AB having y-disp (-: STAB-SWEEP-BACK))))


;;; cone descriptor for PORT-ENGINE (and STARBOARD-ENGINE)

(define cone PEC having
    main-cone (define simple-cone having
       cross-section (define cross-section having type circle
                                                 radius ENGINE-RADIUS)
          spine (define spine having type straight length ENGINE-LENGTH)
          sweeping-rule CSW))


;;; cone descriptor for PORT-WING

(define cone PWC having
    main-cone (define simple-cone PW having
       cross-section (define cross-section having
                                 type rectangle
                                 width WING-WIDTH
                                 height WING-THICK)
          spine (define spine WS having
                    type non-perp
                    length WING-LENGTH
                    y-disp WING-SWEEP-BACK
                    z-disp WING-LIFT)
          sweeping-rule (define sweeping-rule having
                                 type linear
                                 ratio WING-RATIO)))
```

```
;;; cone descriptor for STARBOARD-WING

(define cone SWC having
     main-cone (define simple-cone SW just-like PW having
        spine (define spine just-like WS having
                         y-disp (-: WING-SWEEP-BACK)))))
```

The function "define-specialization" defines a restriction node. A "parent" specification places the new restriction node in the restriciion lattice below the one specified. In general, restrictions can be specified with more than one supremum, but not in this input language. The "specialization-of" specification provides a pointer to a geometric model — i.e. something defined as an "object". Restrictions inherit this from their parent node if not otherwise specified.

```
;;; model hierachy
;;; classes:

(define-specialization GENERIC-JET-AIRCRAFT having
                       specialization-of JET-AIRCRAFT)

(define-specialization L-1011 having
                       parent GENERIC-JET-AIRCRAFT)

(define-specialization BOEING-747 having
                       parent GENERIC-JET-AIRCRAFT)

(define-specialization BOEING-747B having
                       parent BOEING-747)

(define-specialization BOEING-747SP having
                       parent BOEING-747)
```

The constraints for the generic class of wide-bodied passenger jet aircraft are specified below. They constrain the quantifiers used as parameters above. When a constraint is added to a restriction node it is propagated to all the infima (and so on recursively). Thus any constraints added here, are automatically propagated to the subclass L-1011, for instance.

The symbols "≥:" and "≤:" are predicates on two expressions with the obvious meaning. "c-interval" is a predicate on three expressions, exp_1, exp_2 and exp_3 say, implying that $exp_1 \epsilon \, [exp_2, exp_3]$.

```
;;; constraints for GENERIC-JET-AIRCRAFT

;;; the allowable engine configurations
```

```
(constrain GENERIC-JET-AIRCRAFT with
            (c-interval F-ENG-QUANT 1 2)
            (≥: 2 (+: F-ENG-QUANT R-ENG-QUANT))
            (c-interval R-ENG-QUANT 0 1))

;;; allowable sizes

(constrain GENERIC-JET-AIRCRAFT with
            (c-interval FUSELAGE-LENGTH 40.0 70.0)
            (c-interval FUSELAGE-RADIUS 2.5 4.0)
            (c-interval ENGINE-RADIUS 1.0 1.8)
            (c-interval ENGINE-LENGTH 4.0 7.0)
            (c-interval REAR-ENGINE-LENGTH 6.0 10.0)
            (c-interval WING-LENGTH 22 33.5)
            (c-interval (%: WING-LENGTH FUSELAGE-LENGTH) 0.43 0.65)
            (c-interval WING-SWEEP-BACK 13 18)
            (c-interval WING-LIFT 1 2)
            (c-interval WING-WIDTH 7 12)
            (≤: (*: 2 WING-WIDTH) WING-LENGTH)
            (c-interval WING-THICK 1.5 2.5)
            (c-interval WING-RATIO 0.35 0.45)
            (c-interval RUDDER-X-WIDTH 0.7 1.1)
            (c-interval RUDDER-X-HEIGHT 7 13)
            (c-interval RUDDER-LENGTH 8.5 14.2)
            (c-interval RUDDER-SWEEP-BACK 3 9)
            (c-interval RUDDER-RATIO 0.3 0.4)
            (c-interval STAB-WIDTH 5 11)
            (c-interval STAB-THICK 0.7 1.1)
            (c-interval STAB-LENGTH 7.6 13.0)
            (c-interval STAB-SWEEP-BACK 3 7)
            (c-interval STAB-RATIO 0.2 0.55))

;;; allowable affixment ranges

(constrain GENERIC-JET-AIRCRAFT with
            (c-interval WING-ATTACHMENT 20.0 40.0)
            (c-interval WING-ATTACHMENT
                        (*: 0.4 FUSELAGE-LENGTH)
                        (*: 0.6 FUSELAGE-LENGTH))
            (c-interval ENG-OUT 5.0 12.0)
            (c-interval R-ENG-ATTACHMENT 3.0 5.0)
            (c-interval STAB-ATTACH 3.0 5.0)
            (c-interval ENG-GAP 7 10)
            (c-interval ENG-DISP 0 4)
            (c-interval ENG-DISP-GAP 6 10))
```

Now we add the constraints for the sub–class BOEING-747 and its two sub–classes BOEING-747B and BOEING-747SP.

```
;;; constraints for BOEING-747
;;; not quite specific

;;; the engine configuration - two on each wing, none at the back
```

```
(constrain BOEING-747 with
        (=: F-ENG-QUANT 2)
        (=: R-ENG-QUANT 0))

;;; sizes

(constrain BOEING-747 with
        (c-interval FUSELAGE-LENGTH 50.0 70.0)
        (=: FUSELAGE-RADIUS 3.25)
        (=: ENGINE-RADIUS 1.5)
        (=: ENGINE-LENGTH 6.3)
        (=: WING-LENGTH 31.89)
        (=: WING-SWEEP-BACK 17.55)
        (=: WING-LIFT 2.0)
        (=: WING-WIDTH 10.0)
        (=: WING-THICK 2.0)
        (=: WING-RATIO 0.377)
        (=: RUDDER-X-WIDTH 1.0)
        (=: RUDDER-X-HEIGHT 11.73)
        (=: RUDDER-LENGTH 12.6)
        (=: RUDDER-SWEEP-BACK 7.9)
        (=: RUDDER-RATIO (%: 3.99 11.70))
        (=: STAB-WIDTH 9.85)
        (=: STAB-THICK 1.0)
        (=: STAB-LENGTH 11.35)
        (=: STAB-SWEEP-BACK (-: 12.82 (*: 0.5 (+: STAB-WIDTH 2.46))))
        (=: STAB-RATIO (%: 2.46 9.85)))

;;; affixment variables

(constrain BOEING-747 with
        (c-interval WING-ATTACHMENT 27 40)
        (=: ENG-OUT (-: 12.11 FUSELAGE-RADIUS))
        (=: ENG-GAP (-: 21.27 12.11))
        (=: ENG-DISP 3.06)
        (=: ENG-DISP-GAP 8.71)
        (=: STAB-ATTACH 4.9))

;;; extra constraints for BOEING-747B

(constrain BOEING-747B with
        (=: WING-ATTACHMENT 39.95)
        (=: FUSELAGE-LENGTH 67.3))    ;this may well be the length of a
                                      ;standard 747 -- it is sort of made up

;;; extra constraints for BOEING-747SP

(constrain BOEING-747SP with
        (=: WING-ATTACHMENT 27.45)
        (=: FUSELAGE-LENGTH 52.0))    ;made up!
```

The following adds the constraints for the subclass of L-1011s. For this class every quantifier is completely specified.

```
;;; constraints for L-1011
;;; currently specific

;;; the engine configuration - one on each wing, one at the back

(constrain L-1011 with
          (=: F-ENG-QUANT 1)
          (=: R-ENG-QUANT 1))

;;; sizes

(constrain L-1011 with
          (=: FUSELAGE-LENGTH 52.8)
          (=: FUSELAGE-RADIUS 3.0)
          (=: ENGINE-RADIUS 1.4)
          (=: ENGINE-LENGTH 5.3)
          (=: REAR-ENGINE-LENGTH 8.0)
          (=: WING-LENGTH 25.1)
          (=: WING-SWEEP-BACK 14.3)
          (=: WING-LIFT 1.0)
          (=: WING-WIDTH 7.5)
          (=: WING-THICK 2.0)
          (=: WING-RATIO 0.4444444)
          (=: RUDDER-X-WIDTH 0.8)
          (=: RUDDER-X-HEIGHT 8.3)
          (=: RUDDER-LENGTH 10.3)
          (=: RUDDER-SWEEP-BACK 4.8)
          (=: RUDDER-RATIO 0.31)
          (=: STAB-WIDTH 6.4)
          (=: STAB-THICK 0.8)
          (=: STAB-LENGTH 9.5)
          (=: STAB-SWEEP-BACK 4.0)
          (=: STAB-RATIO 0.5))

;;; affixment variables

(constrain L-1011 with
          (=: WING-ATTACHMENT 24.0)
          (=: ENG-OUT 7.6)
          (=: ENG-DISP 0.3)
          (=: R-ENG-ATTACHMENT 4.0)
          (=: STAB-ATTACH 3.2))
```

Instances of generic aircraft are placed in the world at unknown position on the ground and with a rotational degree of freedom about the vertical axis. Recall that the numbers used in the "user-variable" clauses are merely defaults for the graphics module. There are no constraints placed on the three quantifiers introduced here.

```
;;; place things in the world - use meters

(user-variable AIRCRAFT-X -30.0)
```

```
(user-variable AIRCRAFT-Y -20.0)
(user-variable AIRCRAFT-ORI π/4)

(put JET-AIRCRAFT instance-of GENERIC-JET-AIRCRAFT with
    ori AIRCRAFT-ORI about ZHAT
    pos AIRCRAFT-X AIRCRAFT-Y 0)
```

Finally the following code defines a camera looking downwards from a height in the range [1000, 12000]. The focal ratio of the camera is specified to be 20.0.

```
;;; camera model parameters

(user-variable HEIGHT 2000.0)

(constrain with
        (c-interval HEIGHT 1000 12000))

(define camera CAM having fr 20.0)

(camera-put CAM with pos 0 0 HEIGHT)
```

1.3 Models of Small Electric Motors.

Chapter 4 used a class of small electric motors as an example. The following is the input to ACRONYM used to specify the subclasses of motors and instances shown in figure figure 4.5 . The subclass hierarchy was illustrated in figure 4.7 .

The first section of code builds the geometric model of electric motors. Recall that the numbers following user-variable declarations are purely for graphics default purposes.

```
;;; geometric aspects of electric motor

(user-variable MOTOR-RADIUS 3.0)
(user-variable MOTOR-LENGTH 8.0)
(user-variable SPINDLE-RADIUS 0.2)
(user-variable SPINDLE-LENGTH 3.0)
(user-variable FLANGE-QUANTITY 4)
(user-variable FLANGE-HEIGHT 0.25)
(user-variable FLANGE-WIDTH 0.75)
(user-variable FLANGE-LENGTH 1.0)
(user-variable BASE-QUANTITY 0)
(user-variable BASE-WIDTH 5.0)
(user-variable BASE-THICKNESS 0.2)
(user-variable BASE-LENGTH 6.0)


(define object ELECTRIC-MOTOR having
```

```
subpart SPINDLE
subpart (spq FLANGE-QUANTITY of FLANGE-FRAME)
subpart (spq BASE-QUANTITY of BASE)
cone-descriptor (define cone having main-cone
                 (define simple-cone having
                         cross-section (define cross-section having
                                        type CIRCLE
                                        radius MOTOR-RADIUS)
                         spine (define spine having
                                       type STRAIGHT
                                       length MOTOR-LENGTH)
                         sweeping-rule CSW)))

(define object SPINDLE having
  cone-descriptor (define cone having main-cone
                   (define simple-cone having
                           cross-section (define cross-section having
                                          type CIRCLE
                                          radius SPINDLE-RADIUS)
                           spine (define spine having
                                         type STRAIGHT
                                         length SPINDLE-LENGTH)
                           sweeping-rule CSW)))

(affix SPINDLE to ELECTRIC-MOTOR with pos MOTOR-LENGTH 0 0)

(define object FLANGE-FRAME having
  subpart FLANGE)

(define object FLANGE having
  cone-descriptor (define cone having main-cone
                   (define simple-cone having
                           cross-section (define cross-section having
                                          type RECTANGLE
                                          width FLANGE-WIDTH
                                          height FLANGE-HEIGHT)
                           spine (define spine having
                                         type STRAIGHT
                                         length FLANGE-LENGTH)
                           sweeping-rule CSW)))

(user-variable I 1)      ;iteration variable
(affix-iterate FLANGE-FRAME to ELECTRIC-MOTOR
               with pos (-: MOTOR-LENGTH (%: FLANGE-HEIGHT 2)) 0 0
                    ori (-: (%: (*: (-: I 1) 2π) FLANGE-QUANTITY)
                         (*: π 0.25))
                         about XHAT
               over I
               upto FLANGE-QUANTITY)

(affix FLANGE to FLANGE-FRAME
       with pos 0 0 (-: MOTOR-RADIUS)
            ori π%2 about YHAT)
```

```
(define object BASE having
  cone-descriptor (define cone having main-cone
                    (define simple-cone having
                      cross-section (define cross-section having
                                      type RECTANGLE
                                      width BASE-WIDTH
                                      height BASE-THICKNESS)
                      spine (define spine having
                              type STRAIGHT
                              length BASE-LENGTH)
                      sweeping-rule CSW)))

(affix-iterate BASE to ELECTRIC-MOTOR
   with pos (%: (-: MOTOR-LENGTH BASE-LENGTH) 2)
            0
            (-: (+: MOTOR-RADIUS (%: BASE-THICKNESS 2)))
        over I
        upto BASE-QUANTITY)
```

Now we set up the model hierarchy as shown in figure 4.7 .

```
;;; model hierachy
;;; classes:

(define-specialization GENERIC-ELECTRIC-MOTOR having
                       specialization-of ELECTRIC-MOTOR)

(define-specialization MOTOR-WITH-FLANGES having
                       parent GENERIC-ELECTRIC-MOTOR)

(define-specialization MOTOR-WITH-BASE having
                       parent GENERIC-ELECTRIC-MOTOR)

(define-specialization INDUSTRIAL-MOTOR having
                       parent MOTOR-WITH-FLANGES)

(define-specialization GAS-PUMP having
                       parent MOTOR-WITH-FLANGES)

(define-specialization CARBONATOR-MOTOR having
                       parent MOTOR-WITH-BASE)

;;; a few specific instances

(define-specialization INDUSTRIAL-MOTOR-1 having
                       parent INDUSTRIAL-MOTOR)

(define-specialization GAS-PUMP-1 having
                       parent GAS-PUMP)

(define-specialization CARBONATOR-MOTOR-1 having
                       parent CARBONATOR-MOTOR)
```

The following three expressions define the constraints for the generic class of motors, and for the two subclasses distnguished by having a base or having flanges.

```
;;; constraints for GENERIC-ELECTRIC-MOTOR

(constrain GENERIC-ELECTRIC-MOTOR with
          (c-interval MOTOR-LENGTH 6 9)
          (c-interval MOTOR-RADIUS 1.5 3)
          (c-interval (*: MOTOR-LENGTH MOTOR-RADIUS) 12 16)
          (c-interval BASE-QUANTITY 0 1)
          (c-interval FLANGE-QUANTITY 0 6)
          (c-interval SPINDLE-RADIUS 0.25 0.75)
          (c-interval SPINDLE-LENGTH 0.375 2.5))

;;; constraints for MOTOR-WITH-FLANGES and MOTOR-WITH-BASE

(constrain MOTOR-WITH-FLANGES with
          (=: BASE-QUANTITY 0)
          (=: BASE-THICKNESS 0.0)
          (c-interval FLANGE-QUANTITY 3 6))

(constrain MOTOR-WITH-BASE with
          (=: BASE-QUANTITY 1)
          (=: FLANGE-QUANTITY 0)
          (≥: BASE-LENGTH 0.0)
          (≤: BASE-LENGTH MOTOR-LENGTH))
```

Finally more particular subclasses are defined, then even stronger constraints are used to specialize each quantifier to a specific numeric value to produce three specific "instances" of electric motors. These instances were pictured in figure 4.5 .

```
;;; extra constraints for INDUSTRIAL-MOTOR and INDUSTRIAL-MOTOR-1

(constrain INDUSTRIAL-MOTOR with
          (=: FLANGE-QUANTITY 4)
          (c-interval MOTOR-RADIUS 2 3)
          (c-interval MOTOR-LENGTH 6 7.5)
          (=: SPINDLE-RADIUS 0.25)
          (c-interval SPINDLE-LENGTH 1 2.5)
          (c-interval FLANGE-HEIGHT 0.75 1.25)
          (≤: FLANGE-WIDTH FLANGE-HEIGHT)
          (≤: FLANGE-LENGTH FLANGE-WIDTH)
          (≥: FLANGE-LENGTH 0.5))

(constrain INDUSTRIAL-MOTOR-1 with
          (=: MOTOR-RADIUS 2.5)
          (=: MOTOR-LENGTH 6.0)
          (=: SPINDLE-LENGTH 1.5)
          (=: FLANGE-HEIGHT 1.0)
          (=: FLANGE-WIDTH 0.8)
          (=: FLANGE-LENGTH 0.6))

;;; extra constraints for GAS-PUMP and GAS-PUMP-1

(constrain GAS-PUMP with
```

```
                    (=: FLANGE-QUANTITY 3)
                    (c-interval MOTOR-RADIUS 1.5 2)
                    (c-interval MOTOR-LENGTH 7 9)
                    (=: SPINDLE-RADIUS 0.25)
                    (c-interval SPINDLE-LENGTH 0.375 0.625)
                    (c-interval FLANGE-HEIGHT 0.5 0.75)
                    (c-interval FLANGE-WIDTH (*: 2 FLANGE-HEIGHT) (*: 3 FLANGE-HEIGHT))
                    (≤: FLANGE-LENGTH FLANGE-HEIGHT))

(constrain GAS-PUMP-1 with
                    (=: MOTOR-RADIUS 1.5)
                    (=: MOTOR-LENGTH 8.0)
                    (=: SPINDLE-LENGTH 0.5)
                    (=: FLANGE-HEIGHT 0.6)
                    (=: FLANGE-WIDTH 1.5)
                    (=: FLANGE-LENGTH 0.5))

;;; extra constraints for CARBONATOR-MOTOR and CARBONATOR-MOTOR-1

(constrain CARBONATOR-MOTOR with
                    (c-interval BASE-LENGTH (*: (%: 2 3) MOTOR-LENGTH) MOTOR-LENGTH)
                    (c-interval BASE-WIDTH MOTOR-RADIUS (*: 2 MOTOR-RADIUS))
                    (c-interval BASE-THICKNESS 0.125 0.25)
                    (c-interval MOTOR-RADIUS 2 3)
                    (c-interval MOTOR-LENGTH 6 7.5)
                    (=: SPINDLE-RADIUS 0.75)
                    (c-interval SPINDLE-LENGTH 0.375 0.75))

(constrain CARBONATOR-MOTOR-1 with
                    (=: MOTOR-RADIUS 2.5)
                    (=: MOTOR-LENGTH 6.0)
                    (=: SPINDLE-LENGTH 0.5)
                    (=: BASE-LENGTH 5.0)
                    (=: BASE-WIDTH 5.0)
                    (=: BASE-THICKNESS 0.2))
```

1.4 Models for the Insertion Task.

Section 5.5 concerned an example from appendix E of Russell Taylors's dissertation [58]. This section gives the complete parser input to model the situation in the work station. The models are more detailed than those used by Taylor in order that figure 5.6 could be automatically generated. Some inconsistencies in Taylor's presentation of the models have been eliminated.

Taylor freely mixed units of inches and centimeters, and used degrees for radial measurements. The ACRONYM modeling system is indifferent to units of length, but is based on radians for angles. The following few constants allow units to be included easily in all expression used in modeling, and ease automatic conversion into inches and radians internally.

```
(user-constant INCHES 1)
(user-constant CMS (%: 1.0 2.54))

(user-constant RADIANS 1)
(user-constant DEGREES 0.0174532925)
```

The following code describes a rectangloid box whose coordinate system is in the center of its base, with the *z*-axis vertical. There are four holes located in the top of the box. They are represented as as cylinders of zero length. Their coordinate systems have their *x*-axes pointing vertically downwards. The holes are centered distance HOLE-X from the edges in the box coordinate *x* direction and distance HOLE-Y from the edges in the *y* direction.

```
;;; build the box

(user-constant BOX-X (*: 10.00 CMS))
(user-constant BOX-Y (*: 9.00 CMS))
(user-constant BOX-Z (*: 4.90 CMS))

(user-constant HOLE-RADIUS (*: 0.25 INCHES))

(user-constant HOLE-X (*: 1.15 CMS))
(user-constant HOLE-Y (*: 1.30 CMS))

(define object BOX having
  subpart HOLE1
  subpart HOLE2
  subpart HOLE3
  subpart HOLE4
  subpart BOX-VOL)

(define object BOX-VOL having
  cone-descriptor
      (define cone having main-cone
              (define simple-cone having
                      cross-section (define cross-section having
                                            type RECTANGLE
                                            width BOX-Y
                                            height BOX-Z)
                      spine (define spine having
                                    type STRAIGHT
                                    length BOX-X)
                      sweeping-rule CSW)))

(define object HOLE1 having cone-descriptor
      (define cone having main-cone
```

```
(define simple-cone having
    cross-section (define cross-section having
                      type CIRCLE
                      radius HOLE-RADIUS)
    spine (define spine having
              type STRAIGHT
              length 0.0)
    sweeping-rule CSW)))
```

```
(define object HOLE2 just-like HOLE1)
(define object HOLE3 just-like HOLE1)
(define object HOLE4 just-like HOLE1)
```

```
(affix BOX-VOL to BOX with
    pos (-: (%: BOX-X 2)) 0 (%: BOX-Z 2))
```

```
(affix HOLE1 to BOX-VOL with
    pos HOLE-X (-: (-: (%: BOX-Y 2) HOLE-Y)) (%: BOX-Z 2)
    ori π%2 about YHAT)
```

```
(affix HOLE2 to BOX-VOL with
    pos HOLE-X (-: (%: BOX-Y 2) HOLE-Y) (%: BOX-Z 2)
    ori π%2 about YHAT)
```

```
(affix HOLE3 to BOX-VOL with
    pos (-: BOX-X HOLE-X) (-: (-: (%: BOX-Y 2) HOLE-Y)) (%: BOX-Z 2)
    ori π%2 about YHAT)
```

```
(affix HOLE4 to BOX-VOL with
    pos (-: BOX-X HOLE-X) (-: (%: BOX-Y 2) HOLE-Y) (%: BOX-Z 2)
    ori π%2 about YHAT)
```

The box is placed in the world on the work table — the z coordinate is zero. Its orientation about the vertical axis is also given. There are three degrees of potential error in its placement: two in its position on the table, and one in its orientation. Three quantifiers are introduced to model these errors, namely BOX-DELTA-POS-X, BOX-DELTA-POS-Y and BOX-DELTA-ORI. They are constrained later. The defaults given here for quantifiers are for the benefit of the graphics module in case it can't deduce specific default values for the quantifiers by some other method. The numbers are not par of the model.

```
;;; put the box in the world
```

```
(user-variable BOX-POS-X (*: 18.0 INCHES))
(user-variable BOX-POS-Y (*: 40.0 INCHES))
(user-variable BOX-ORI 0.0)
```

```
(user-variable BOX-DELTA-POS-X 0.0)
(user-variable BOX-DELTA-POS-Y 0.0)
```

```
(user-variable BOX-DELTA-ORI 0.0)

(put BOX with
     pos (+: BOX-POS-X BOX-DELTA-POS-X) (+: BOX-POS-Y BOX-DELTA-POS-Y) 0
     ori (+: BOX-ORI BOX-DELTA-ORI) about ZHAT)
```

Next a class of screwdrivers is modeled. They have length ranging between 1 and 10 inches.

```
;;; the screwdriver - between one and ten inches long

(user-variable DRIVER-LENGTH (*: 10.0 INCHES))
(user-variable HANDLE-LENGTH (*: 4.0 INCHES))

(constrain with
        (c-interval DRIVER-LENGTH (*: 1.0 INCHES) (*: 10.0 INCHES))
        (=: HANDLE-LENGTH (*: 0.4 DRIVER-LENGTH)))

(user-constant HANDLE-RADIUS (*: 0.5 INCHES))
(user-constant SHAFT-RADIUS (*: 0.125 INCHES))

(define object SCREWDRIVER having
   subpart SHAFT
   subpart HANDLE)

(define object HANDLE having cone-descriptor
        (define cone having main-cone
                (define simple-cone having
                        cross-section (define cross-section having
                                              type CIRCLE
                                              radius HANDLE-RADIUS)
                        spine (define spine having
                                     type STRAIGHT
                                     length HANDLE-LENGTH)
                        sweeping-rule CSW)))

(define object SHAFT having cone-descriptor
        (define cone having main-cone
                (define simple-cone having
                        cross-section (define cross-section having
                                              type CIRCLE
                                              radius SHAFT-RADIUS)
                        spine (define spine having
                                     type STRAIGHT
                                     length (-: DRIVER-LENGTH HANDLE-LENGTH))
                        sweeping-rule CSW)))

(affix HANDLE to SCREWDRIVER)
(affix SHAFT to HANDLE with pos HANDLE-LENGTH 0 0)
```

Now a screw is modeled. It has a chamfered head and a pointed tip. It is 1.25 inches long. The top of its head is the same radius as the holes on the surface of the box: 0.25 inches. A null object called TIP-POINT is affixed to the tip of the screw. This is so that ACRONYM's geometric resaoning system can compare the location of the tip of the screwdriver (the origin of TIP-POINT's coordinate system) with the center of the hole into which it is to be inserted (given by the origin of HOLE4's coordinate system).

```
;;; model of the screw

(user-constant SCREW-LENGTH (*: 1.25 INCHES))     ;= 3.175 CMS (Taylor has 3.18)

(user-constant HEAD-LENGTH (*: 0.25 INCHES))
(user-constant SCREW-SHAFT-RADIUS (*: 0.125 INCHES))
(user-constant TIP-LENGTH (*: 0.25 INCHES))

(define object SCREW having
   subpart HEAD
   subpart SCREW-SHAFT)

(define object HEAD having cone-descriptor
        (define cone having main-cone
             (define simple-cone having
                    cross-section (define cross-section having
                                          type CIRCLE
                                          radius HOLE-RADIUS)
                    spine (define spine having
                                 type STRAIGHT
                                 length HEAD-LENGTH)
                    sweeping-rule (define sweeping-rule having
                                         type LINEAR
                                         ratio (%: SCREW-SHAFT-RADIUS
                                                   HOLE-RADIUS)))))

(define object SCREW-SHAFT having
   cone-descriptor (define cone having main-cone
                         (define simple-cone having
                                cross-section (define cross-section having
                                                      type CIRCLE
                                                      radius SCREW-SHAFT-RADIUS)
                                spine (define spine having
                                             type STRAIGHT
                                             length (-: SCREW-LENGTH
                                                        (+: HEAD-LENGTH
                                                            TIP-LENGTH)))
                                sweeping-rule CSW))
   subpart TIP)

(define object TIP having cone-descriptor
        (define cone having main-cone
             (define simple-cone having
                    cross-section (define cross-section having
                                          type CIRCLE
                                          radius SCREW-SHAFT-RADIUS)
                    spine (define spine having
                                 type STRAIGHT
                                 length TIP-LENGTH)
```

```
sweeping-rule (define sweeping-rule having
                type LINEAR
                ratio 0.0))))

(affix HEAD to SCREW)
(affix SCREW-SHAFT to HEAD with pos HEAD-LENGTH 0 0)
(affix TIP to SCREW-SHAFT with
       pos (-: SCREW-LENGTH (+: HEAD-LENGTH TIP-LENGTH)) 0 0)
(affix TIP-POINT to TIP with pos TIP-LENGTH 0 0)
```

Now the hand of the arm is defined. This is a null object. Only its coordinate frame is modeled. The hand is placed at a point in three space, with three degrees of positional uncertainty given by HAND-DELTA-POS-X, HAND-DELTA-POS-Y and HAND-DELTA-POZ-Z. Then another null object, FINGERS, is attached to the hand frame, via three degrees of rotational freedom given by HAND-WOBBLE-X, HAND-WOBBLE-Y and HAND-WOBBLE-Z. Recall again the the numbers given here following declarations of variable names are purely for graphics defaults, and not part of the models.

```
;;; the hand and its place in the world and attach three degrees of wobble

(user-variable HAND-POS-X (*: 49.57 CMS))
(user-variable HAND-POS-Y (*: 104.8 CMS))
(user-variable HAND-POS-Z (+: BOX-Z SCREW-LENGTH (*: 10.0 INCHES)))

(user-variable HAND-DELTA-POS-X 0.0)
(user-variable HAND-DELTA-POS-Y 0.0)
(user-variable HAND-DELTA-POS-Z 0.0)

(define object HAND)

(put HAND with
     pos (+: HAND-POS-X HAND-DELTA-POS-X)
         (+: HAND-POS-Y HAND-DELTA-POS-Y)
         (+: HAND-POS-Z HAND-DELTA-POS-Z)
     ori π about YHAT)

;;; now attach the fingers (grasp point) via three degrees of wobble.
;;; this is to model three degrees of freedom in the orientation of the hand.

(user-variable HAND-WOBBLE-Z 0.0)
(user-variable HAND-WOBBLE-Y 0.0)
(user-variable HAND-WOBBLE-X 0.0)

(affix WOBBLE1 to HAND with ori HAND-WOBBLE-Z about ZHAT)
(affix WOBBLE2 to WOBBLE1 with ori HAND-WOBBLE-Y about YHAT)
(affix FINGERS to WOBBLE2 with ori HAND-WOBBLE-X about XHAT)
```

The following section of code attaches the screwdriver rigidly to the fingers. The screw is placed at the tip of the screwdriver, but it is allowed two degrees of rotational freedom about axes at the tip of the screwdriver orthogonal to the screwdriver shaft. These freedoms are represented by quantifiers SCREW-WOBBLE-Y and SCREW-WOBBLE-Z.

```
;;; attach driver to hand and screw to driver

;;; make screwdriver point downwards

(affix SCREWDRIVER to FINGERS with ori -π%2 about YHAT)

;;; now have to attach screw to the tip of the screwdriver

(user-variable SCREW-WOBBLE-Y 0.0)
(user-variable SCREW-WOBBLE-Z 0.0)

(affix SWOBBLE to SCREWDRIVER with
       pos DRIVER-LENGTH 0 0
       ori SCREW-WOBBLE-Y about YHAT)
(affix SCREW to SWOBBLE with ori SCREW-WOBBLE-Z about ZHAT)
```

The remainder of the code is devoted to constraining all the quantifiers to model a particular spatial set up, with varying amounts of error in the position and orientation parameters.

A restriction node NOMINAL is introduced to model the nominal spatial location and orientation of all the objects in the world.

The box is placed in the world, at world coordinates (18, 40, 0). This is right in the center of the working area of the Stanford *blue arm* as set up at the Stanford Artificial Intelligence Laboratory. These are the coordinates Taylor used. It also has a nominal orientation lining up with the table coordinate axes.

The hand is given a nominal position such that with no errors in the system, the tip of the screw will be exactly at the center of the hole. Furthermore the hand is known to have position errors bounded by ±0.05 inches in all three coordinates, and ±0.025 degrees in three orientations.

```
;;; constraints to set up the nominal positions and hand errors

(define-specialization NOMINAL having specialization-of SITUATION)

(constrain NOMINAL with
           (=: BOX-POS-X (*: 18.0 INCHES))
           (=: BOX-POS-Y (*: 40.0 INCHES))
           (=: BOX-ORI 0.0))
```

```
(constrain NOMINAL with
        (=: HAND-POS-X (+: BOX-POS-X (%: BOX-X 2) (-: HOLE-X)))
        (=: HAND-POS-Y (+: BOX-POS-Y (%: BOX-Y 2) (-: HOLE-Y)))
        (=: HAND-POS-Z (+: BOX-Z SCREW-LENGTH DRIVER-LENGTH)))

(constrain NOMINAL with
        (c-interval HAND-DELTA-POS-X (*: -0.05 INCHES) (*: 0.05 INCHES))
        (c-interval HAND-DELTA-POS-Y (*: -0.05 INCHES) (*: 0.05 INCHES))
        (c-interval HAND-DELTA-POS-Z (*: -0.05 INCHES) (*: 0.05 INCHES)))

(constrain NOMINAL with
        (c-interval HAND-WOBBLE-Z (*: -0.25 DEGREES) (*: 0.25 DEGREES))
        (c-interval HAND-WOBBLE-Y (*: -0.25 DEGREES) (*: 0.25 DEGREES))
        (c-interval HAND-WOBBLE-X (*: -0.25 DEGREES) (*: 0.25 DEGREES)))
```

The restriction node TAYLOR is introduced to model the situation exactly as Taylor described it. The screwdriver is exactly 10 inches long and the box has position errors of ± 0.3 inches in one direction, ± 0.2 in another, and a rotational error of ± 5 degrees. The screw is allowed to wobble ± 5 degrees in two directions at the end of the screwdriver.

```
;;; constraints to match Taylor's example

(define-specialization TAYLOR having parent NOMINAL)

(constrain TAYLOR with (=: DRIVER-LENGTH 10.0))

(constrain TAYLOR with
        (c-interval BOX-DELTA-POS-X (*: -0.3 INCHES) (*: 0.3 INCHES))
        (c-interval BOX-DELTA-POS-Y (*: -0.2 INCHES) (*: 0.2 INCHES))
        (c-interval BOX-DELTA-ORI (*: -5 DEGREES) (*: 5 DEGREES)))

(constrain TAYLOR with
        (c-interval SCREW-WOBBLE-Y (*: -5 DEGREES) (*: 5 DEGREES))
        (c-interval SCREW-WOBBLE-Z (*: -5 DEGREES) (*: 5 DEGREES)))
```

The last example used somewhat tighter constraints for the box position, and the screw wobble. They are given here attached to a specialization EXAMPLE of NOMINAL.

```
;;; additional constraints for tool selection

(define-specialization EXAMPLE having parent NOMINAL)

(constrain EXAMPLE with
        (c-interval BOX-DELTA-POS-X (*: -0.05 INCHES) (*: 0.05 INCHES))
        (c-interval BOX-DELTA-POS-Y (*: -0.05 INCHES) (*: 0.05 INCHES))
        (c-interval BOX-DELTA-ORI (*: -0.5 DEGREES) (*: 0.5 DEGREES)))

(constrain EXAMPLE with
        (c-interval SCREW-WOBBLE-Y (*: -2 DEGREES) (*: 2 DEGREES))
        (c-interval SCREW-WOBBLE-Z (*: -2 DEGREES) (*: 2 DEGREES)))
```

These constraints were used to determine contraints on DRIVER-LENGTH if the screw is to inserted in the hole successfully.

Appendix 2

Low Level Descriptive Process

Section 9.1 described some results of ACRONYM interpreting aerial images. The low level descriptive processes used for those experiments were implemented as two modules. The first, described in the next section, is completely bottom–up, and run on images as a preprocessing step. The second, described in section A2.2 receives guidance from the prediction graph, and is run at the same time as the rest of ACRONYM (but in a separate core image — chapter 3 contains details).

2.1 The Nevatia–Babu Line Finder.

The pre-processing line finder was written by Ramakant Nevatia and Ramesh Babu [46] at USC and transported to Stanford by Mike Lowry.

It determines edge magnitude and direction by using edge masks in six different directions. These are thinned and subjected to a threshold, then linked, based on proximity and orientation. The linked elements are approximated by piecewise straight line segments. Each line segment has a direction associated with it, and a consistent side has the brighter intensity.

2.2 The Ribbon and Ellispe Finder.

We refer to the module which finds ribbons and ellipses as PEMM for Prototype Edge Mapping Module. The following description of PEMM is a modified version of Brooks [20].

The PEMM is guided by a PEMM-program. It consists of three sets of heuristics and a number of parameter values. In ACRONYM the prediction algorithms produce a PEMM-program simultaneously as they produce the prediction graph. The first section below describes PEMM itself and the second describes the actual heauristics which are available for selection for a PEMM-program.

2.2.1 The Prototype Edge Mapping Module.

There are three relatively independent phases of the algorithm; linking edges into candidate contours, discarding unsatisfactory candidates, and finally finding ribbon and ellipse descriptions for contours and the regions they bound. We discuss these three phases in order below.

Linking edges into a contour can easily be formulated as a tree searching problem. Each node is an ordered list of edge elements, with a score attached giving a measure of goodness of the contour specified by the list. There is also an optional direction. Recall that the edge elements are directed so that their right sides are brighter than their left. A direction of "right" will be interpreted to mean that the edge list is following around a relatively brighter region, and "left" a darker region. The root node of the tree is a list of a single edge element. A descendent node m of a node n with edge list $e_{n_1}, e_{n_2}, \ldots, e_{n_k}$ will have edge list $e_{n_1}, e_{n_2}, \ldots, e_{n_k}, e_{n_{k+1}}$; i.e. each descendent node extends the contour by one new edge element. If a node has a direction, then its descendent nodes have the same direction. In its most general form, each node has a descendent for every edge element in the image which is not already on its edge list. To find the best contour starting with a given edge element we must search the tree to find the node with the best score.

There are four issues to resolve for such a tree search.

1. Which edges should be chosen as root nodes of search trees?

2. The tree as defined will clearly be enormous (of size $(n-1)!$ where n is typically 500 to 1000). Therefore the tree must be pruned, and not all nodes searched. How should this be done?

3. What scoring function should be used?

4. In what order should the tree be searched and when should the search be terminated?

The solutions to these four problems incorporate a capability for the PEMM–program to direct the contour finding process.

The PEMM–program can restrict the edges which will be used as root nodes to some sub–area of the image. This is useful when there has already been a partial interpretation of the image, and the search for more details of a hypothesized object can be severely limited. Additionally the PEMM–program may include a length threshold to elimate basing search trees on noise edges.

We use a best–first search algorithm to search partially a sub–tree of the total search tree. The sub–tree which may actually be searched is defined by two lists of heuristics provided by the PEMM-program; the *producers* and the *reapers*. As we will see below, the ordering of producers is important for the order in which the search tree is traversed, and so in the case of incomplete search (the normal case), this ordering can affect the search outcome. The ordering of reapers can affect the efficiency of the search but not the outcome. The depth first search, combined with the scoring function determines the search order.

A best first tree search algorithm works as follows. A list of nodes is kept in decreasing order of their score. Initially the list contains only the root node, which is assigned score zero. A node is said to be fully developed if all its descendents in the sub–tree defined by the producers and reapers have already been placed on the the ordered node list. A node is partially developed if it is not fully developed. Best–first search finds the first partially developed node on the ordered list (i.e. the partially developed node with the highest score), calculates another descendent and its score, and inserts the new node into the list. This continues until there are n_nodes (a parameter supplied by the PEMM-program) fully developed at the head of the list. The result of the search is the edge list associated with the node at the head of the list, which will be the highest scoring node found during the search. Note that a node can never be promoted on the ordered list. Further, the search for a node to develop will never proceed past the first n_nodes, for then there would have to n_nodes fully developed, and so the tree search would terminate. Thus only the first n_nodes of the ordered list need be retained.

The producers are functions of an edge element and a direction, used to produce descendents of a node. They are applied to the most recent edge of a node, and the node's direction. A producer returns a list of descendents, and a score for each of those edges. When the search procedure wants to develop a node, by finding another descendent, it checks to see if there are any edges left from the last producer used. If not it calls the next producer. It continues until it has an edge element which is neither already in the contour, nor has been previously suggested by a producer. It also demands that if the parent node had an associated direction, the exterior angle made by the new edge element is within slop degrees of continuing in that direction (slop is a parameter supplied by the PEMM-program). Finally the search procedure tests the proposed new edge element with the predicates in the reapers list. These are predicates of edge list from the parent node, the proposed new edge and the direction of the parent node. When the search procedure finally has a new edge, it makes up a new node, with that edge added to the contour, and a score from the parent node, incremented by the score associated with the new edge, weighted by its length.

Thus the decisions about which edges to link are mostly made on the basis of very local information, namely the previous edge linked, and the general rotational direction of the contour. For small values of slop the contours tend to encompass almost convex regions.

The second phase is rather simple. Since the contours are found using only very local properties of the edge elements, it is necessary to make more global checks before proceeding to fit ribbon descriptions. The PEMM-prog suppliea a list of predicates, *cullers*, which each take two arguments; a contour and the direction used in finding that contour. A candidate contour is retained only if it and its associated direction satisfy all the predicates in cullers. Note that these predicates too may be parameterized by global variables set by the PEMM-program. Also, the ordering of cullers cannot affect the final outcome, but it can affect efficiency.

The final phase is fitting ribbon and ellipse descriptions to the contours. Ribbons are planar area descriptors which are the two dimensional specialization of generalized cones. We use a subset of the general definition of the class of all ribbons. In particular, they must be defined by sweeping a symmetric width element normally along a straight spine while changing the width linearly with distance swept. We will call the two lines defined by the width element as it is swept along the spine, ribbon edges. Thus the ribbons we use can be fully specified by a line segment (the spine) and a width at each end. An ellipse is defined by the lengths of orthogonal major and minor axes. Both ribbons and ellipses have an orientation within an image. A ribbon's orientation is defined by the direction of its spine, and the orientation of an ellipse by that of its major axis. Fitting of ribbons and ellipses contours is done by a fixed algorithm with no mechanism for goal direction from the PEMM-program.

Fitting a ribbon proceeds as follows. A histogram of the angles of the edge elements making up the contour (weighted for edge length) is constructed at 20 degree intervals. The two peaks with the largest areas, between local minima, are found, and the edge elements which contribute to each are identified. The two edges of the proposed ribbon description are fitted to these collections of edge elements. First the mean angles (weighted for edge element length) are calculated, and then straight lines, constrained by these angles are fitted by least squares, weighted by length once again. The line whose angle is the mean of the ribbon edge angles, and which is equidistant from the ribbon edges, is calculated. The edge elements which defined the ribbon edges are normally projected onto the center line, to define the extremities of the spine. The width function for the ribbon can then be easily calculated from the spine and the ribbon edges.

Fitting an ellipse proceeds as follows. The edges in the contours which do not join their successor are joined by a straight line. The result is a polygon. The center of mass of the polygon is computed. This becomes the center of the ellipse. The point on the polygon furthest from the center is found, and the major axis is defined by this point and the center. The edges in the contour are projected onto the line through the center normal to the major axis and the length of the minor axis is thus calculated.

2.2.2 Library Heuristics.

There is a library of heuristic *producers, reapers* and *cullers*. The PEMM-program selects heauristics from this library.

There are three *producers*. NEXT-SUPSERSEG-MEM follows the linking provided by the line finder of Nevatia and Babu. CONTINUATION looks for an edge which is colinear to the the current one, but perhaps some distance away. This heuristic is selected by the predictor when there is evidence that attached cones will break up the edge of the ribbon of a desired cone. Finally GET-NEARBY looks for edges which happen to begin near the termination of the previous edge. The direction of the current contour is noted in this search.

There are two *reapers*. CHECK-CONVEX-HERE makes sure that adding the proposed edge to the current contour will not introduce a local non-convexity at the place of addition. Similarly CHECK-CONVEX-THERE checks that the new edge does not imply that there must be a non-convexity somewhere between it and a continuation to meet the beginning of the contour.

There are five *cullers* which check completed contours. CHECK-NUM-EDGES check that there are at least some minimum number of edges in the contour. CHECK-EXTERIOR-ANGLES checks that the sum of the exterior angles of the contour is above some threshold. This is a measure of how closed the contour is. CHECK-AREA-ESTIMATE checks the area encompassed by the contour. It must lie within programmable upper and lower bounds. CHECK-BEST-PEAK histograms the angular distribution of edges modulo 180 degrees and checks that the biggest peak is above some threshold in length-weighted proportion of all edges of the contour. CHECK-TWO-PEAKS histograms the angles modulo 360 degress and checks that the best two weighted peaks lie in some specified range of separation. This is a good check that ribbons have the right sweeping ratio.

Appendix 3

The ACRONYM Rule System

The rule system consists of a rule parser–compiler which translates production-like rules into MACLISP functions, and a rule control system which decides which rules should be invoked when. The rule system is used to implement most of prediction and the higher level aspects of interpretation in the ACRONYM system.

3.1 How Rules Work.

The rules are essentially production rules which are invoked by backward chaining.

A rule has three major parts. A set of *pre–conditions*, a *body* and an *advertisment*. The first two are optional. A rule may be invoked by the rule system when its advertisement unifies with a subgoal whose satisfaction is currently desired. All the pre-conditions are evaluated until one returns NIL. If that happens then the rule has failed and another one must be tried to satisfy the subgoal. A pre–condition may set up another subgoal. In that case the current rule is suspended and the rule system recursively tries to get that subgoal satisified. If all the preconditions evaluate to non-NIL the rule is said to fire. The body of the rule is evaluated, and then the advertisement is evaluated. The rule system then considers the original subgoal to have been satisifed. It may happen that multiple values are returned to whatever rule set up that subgoal. There is one final caveat. It is possible that there were extra conditions in the subgoal specification about *how* it should be satsified. If these conditions are not met, more rules are tried in an attempt to satisfactorarily meet the subgoal.

Note also that is is possible to terminate a rule during firing and thus fail to satisfy the subgoal. This is done with the non–local exit macro ABORT-RULE.

The pre–conditions and advertisement must conform to a rigid syntax. The rule body can be arbitrary LISP code. The rule parser–compiler translates the rules into LISP functions, which can then be compiled with the standard MACLISP compiler.

When the rule system has a subgoal is must satisfy it looks for rules whose advertisement might unify with the subgoal. There are various hash tables employed to retrieve only those rules with a good chance of unification. If the subgoal and a rule's advertisement unify (using the algorithm described below) then the rule's pre–conditions are tested. The process is repeated until a rule satisfactorarily fires. There are two exceptions to this strategy however. If the subgoal is of an ASSERT, or LASSERT type then the rule system first looks in some data-bases to see whether the desired assertions have already been made.

The reason for insisting on a rigid syntax for the rules was that it was hoped that *meta–rules* would be able to examine the rule sources to help decide on rule sets capabilities and thus control the rule system better. The ACRONYM rule sets ended up not making use of these capabilities. The rigid syntax and the checking of that syntax by the parser does provide a useful error check on rule definitions however.

3.2 The Unification Algorithm.

For a subgoal specification to invoke a rule, it must be unifiable with the rule's advertisement. We will refer to the expression set up by a π-SUBGOAL predicate as an SG, and a rule's advertisement as an AD.

Both SGs and ADs are lisp lists, i.e. binary trees which have atomic symbols at their leaves. In both cases these symbols can include single question marks, atoms with ? as their first character, and atoms with ∎ as their first character. We will refer to the last two classes as ?vars and ∎vars respectively. The CAR of the expression must be an atom which is neither a ?var, nor a ∎var.

The ?vars are used by both SGs and ADs to ask for values from each other. A ?var in a subgoal indicates that a value for that variable is desired from the rule which satisfies the subgoal. A ?var in an AD indicates that the rule desires a value for that variable before invocation. Single question marks are treated much the same, except that the value is thrown away.

The =vars have slightly different meanings for SGs and ADs. In fact in the case of SGs, they can actually be =s-expressions. A SG evaluates its =s-expressions and splices the values into the pattern in place, before even selecting rules to be unified. An AD evaluates and splices in its =vars after execution of the rule, in order to hand back values to SG ?vars (and to evaluate the AD).

Thus the subgoal (ASSERT COLOR =X =Y) where X has value BLOCKA and Y has value RED will become (ASSERT COLOR BLOCKA RED) before unification is attempted.

Unification proceeds as follows. Both the spliced SG and the AD are binary trees. They are layed on top of each other and compared. They will share a common subtree rooted at their own roots (the root node at the very least!). Their structures diverge when a leaf of one corresponds to the root of a subtree of the other. The following correspondences between leafs and what they match are allowed (note that there is some overlap between the two tables)

Leaf of SG		Subtree of AD
atom	→	atom (must be EQ)
	→	≡πRN (if the context agrees)
?var (inc ?)	→	?–free subtree (includes atoms)

Leaf of AD		Subtree of SG
atom	→	atom (must be EQ)
	→	?var (inc ?)
?var (inc ?)	→	?–free subtree (includes atoms)
≡var	→	?var
≡πRN	→	atom (if the context agrees)

When a ?var in an advertisement is matched, the named variable will be bound to what it matched when the rule is invoked. Similarly when a ?var in a subgoal is matched, the named variable will be bound to what it matched after a rule which satisfies the subgoal has been found and fired. Thus the ? convention can be used to pass multiple arguments and receive multiple return values.

Suppose we have a subgoal expression

$$(\pi\text{-SUBGOAL} \quad (\text{FOO ?BAR (X . ≡Y) ≡BAZ ?A2}))$$

where say Y has value (A B C) and BAZ has value BAZOLA. Then the spliced SG expression becomes

$$(\text{FOO ?BAR (X A B C) BAZOLA ?A2})$$

which unifies with, for example:

AD expression	Invocation bindings	Return bindings
(FOO ≡RES (X ? . ?REST) BAZOLA FOO)	REST ← (B C)	
		BAR ← <value of RES>
		A2 ← FOO
'(FOO (A . ≡B) ?N1 ?N2 ≡R)	N1 ← (X A B C)	
	N2 ← BAZOLA	
		BAR ← (A . <value of B>)
		A2 ← <value of R>

3.3 An Example Rule.

Here is an example of a typical rule taken directly from a source file. It predicts the apparent length of a some image feature (e.g. width of a ribbon, axis length of an ellipse) where the feature being measured has an orientation relative to the camera as described in the comments preceding the rule.

```
;;; single rotation about normal to what is being measured,
;;; axis parallel to image plane. magnitude is between -π/2 and π/2.
;;; can put stronger back constraints on the world if we know that.

(RULE SH-PARAMS-3
     PC (π-SUBGOAL (LASSERT INF-BOUND
                          (≡(ε-SETQ CT (LIST 'COS MAG)) . ≡πRN)
                          ?CL))
        (π-PREDAPPLY 'NUMBERP CL)
        (π-NOT (π-PREDAPPLY 'LESSP CL 0))
        (π-SUBGOAL (LASSERT SUP-BOUND (≡CT . ≡πRN) ?CH))
        (π-PROGN (ε-SETQ EXP
                        (CANONSIMPLIFY πRN
                                      (M%: (M*: PARV FR CT)
                                           (M-: Z))))
                 (ε-SETQ LOEXP
                        (CANONSIMPLIFY πRN
                                      (M%: (M*: PARV FR CL)
                                           (M-: Z))))
                 (ε-SETQ HIEXP
```

```
                    (CANONSIMPLIFY πRN
                                (M%: (M*: PARV FR CH)
                                     (M-: Z)))))
          (π-SUBGOAL '(PREDICT-PEMM-SINGLE-PARAM ≡TYPE ≡PARAM ≡CTR
                                          ≡EXP ≡QP ≡LOEXP ≡HIEXP))
          (π-OR (π-SUBGOAL '(BACK-SOLVE-COSINE ≡QP
                                        ≡MAG
                                        ≡(CANONSIMPLIFY
                                          πRN
                                          (M%: (M*: '●LO (M-: Z))
                                               (M*: PARV FR)))
                                        ≡(CANONSIMPLIFY
                                          πRN
                                          (M%: (M*: '●HI (M-: Z))
                                               (M*: PARV FR)))))
              (ε-PROGN 'T))
          (π-SUBGOAL '(ADD-BACK ≡QP ≡(M≤: '●LO HIEXP)))
          (π-SUBGOAL '(ADD-BACK ≡QP ≡(M≥: '●HI LOEXP)))
      AD '(PREDICT-SINGLE-PARAM ?TYPE
                                (?PARAM ?PARV . ?QP)
                                (?CTR ?Z . ?FR)
                                (FACTOR (COS ?MAG))))
```

The arguments are passed by the unification algorithm through the AD expression. Here TYPE is one of RIBBON or ELLIPSE, PARAM concerns which parameter of the shape is being predicted (e.g. LENGTH), PARV is an expression defining the three-dimensional model paramater that will generate the image feature, QP is a data structure for the prediction, CTR is the model contour from which the predicton is being made, Z is the z camera coordinate of the object, FR is the focal ratio of the camera, and MAG is the expression of the magnitude of the rotation of the object relative to the camera as defined in the comments preceding the rule.

Bibliography

[1]   Abraham, R.G., T. Csakvary, J. Korpela, L. Shum, R.J.S. Stewart, and A. Taleff; *Programmable Assembly Research Technology: Transfer to Industry,* 4th Bi-Monthly Report, NSF Grant ISP 76-24164, Westinghouse R&D Center, Pittsburgh, Penn., June 1977.

[2]   Agin, Gerald J.; *Representation and Description of Curved Objects,* Stanford AI Lab Memo AIM-173, Oct. 1972.

[3]   Agin, Gerald J.; *Hierarchical Representation of Three-dimensional Objects using Verbal Models,* IEEE Transactions on Pattern Analysis and Machine Intelligence, Vol. PAMI-3, No. 2, March 1981.

[4]   Ambler, A.P., and R.J. Popplestone; *Inferring the Positions of Bodies from Specified Spatial Relationships,* Artificial Intelligence 6, 1975, 175-208.

[5]   Baer, Adrian, Charles Eastman, and Max Henrion; *A Survey of Geometric Modeling,* CMU Institute of Physical Planning Research Report No. 66, March 1977.

[6]   Baker, H. Harlyn; *Edge Based Stereo Correlation,* Proceedings ARPA Image Understanding Workshop, College Park, MD, April 1980, 168-175.

[7]   Barrow, Harry G., and Jay M. Tenenbaum; *MSYS: A System for Reasoning About Scenes,* SRI AI Center, Tech. Note 121, March 1976.

[8]   *Recovering Intrinsic Scene Characteristics from Images,* in *Computer Vision Systems,* A. Hanson and E. Riseman eds., Academic Press, New York, 1978, 3-26.

[9]   Baumgart, Bruce G.; *Geometric Modeling for Computer Vision,* Stanford AI Lab Memo AIM—249, Oct. 1974.

[10] Binford, Thomas O.; *Visual Perception by Computer,* Invited paper at IEEE Systems Science and Cybernetics Conference, Miami, Dec. 1971.

[11] Binford, Thomas O.; *Computer Integrated Assembly Systems,* Proceedings NSF Grantees Conference on Industrial Automation, Cornell Univ., Sept. 1979.

[12] Binford, Thomas O.; *Inferring Surfaces from Images,* AI Journal, to appear.

[13] Bledsoe, W.W.; *The Sup-Inf Method in Presburger Arithmetic,* Memo ATP-18, Dept. of Match. and Comp. Sci., University of Texas at Austin, Austin, Texas, Dec. 1974.

[14] Bledsoe, W.W.; *A New Method for Proving Certain Presburger Formulas,* Proceedings of IJCAI-4, Tibilsi, Georgia, U.S.S.R., Sept. 1975, 15-21.

[15] Bobrow, Daniel G.; *Natural Language Input for a Computer Problem Solving System,* in *Semantic Information Processing,* M.L. Minsky ed., MIT Press, 1968.

[16] Bobrow, Daniel G., and Terry Winograd; *An Overview of KRL, a Knowledge Representation Language,* Cognitive Science 1, 1977, 3-46.

[17] Bolles, Robert C.; *Verification Vision Within a Programmable Assembly System,* Stanford AI Lab Memo AIM—295, Dec. 1976.

[18] Borning, Alan; *THINGLAB: A Constraint-Oriented Simulation Laboratory,* Stanford CS Report, STAN-CS-79-746, July 1979.

[19] Braid, I.C.; *Designing With Volumes,* Cantab Press, Cambridge, England, 1973.

[20] Brooks, Rodney A.; *Goal-Directed Edge Linking and Ribbon Finding,* Proceedings ARPA Image Understanding Workshop, Menlo Park, April 1979, 72-76.

[21] Brooks, Rodney A., Russell Greiner, and Thomas O. Binford; *The ACRONYM Model-Based Vision System,* Proceedings IJCAI-6, Tokyo, August 1979, 105-113.

[22] Brooks, Rodney A., and Thomas O. Binford; *Representing and Reasoning About Partially Specified Scenes,* Proceedings ARPA Image Understanding Workshop, College Park, MD, April 1980, 95-103.

[23] Drake, S.; *Using Compliance in Lieu of Sensory Feedback for Automatic Assembly,* Charles Stark Draper Lab. Report T-657, Sept. 1977.

[24] Fikes, Richard E.; *REF-ARF: A System for Solving Problems Stated as Procedures,* Artificial Intelligence 1, 1970, 27-120.

[25] Garvey, Thomas D.; *Perceptual Strategies for Purposive Vision,* SRI AI Center, Tech. Note 117, Sept. 1976.

[26] Goldman, Ron; *Recent Work with the AL System,* Proceedings IJCAI-5, Cambridge, August 1977, 733-735.

[27] Grimson, W.E.L.; *Aspects of a Computational Theory of Human Stereo Vision,* Proceedings ARPA Image Understanding Workshop, College Park, MD, April 1980, 128-149.

[28] Grossman, David D.; *Monte Carlo Simulation of Tolerancing in Discrete Parts Manufacturing and Assembly,* Stanford AI Lab Memo AIM-280, May 1976.

[29] Grossman, David D.; *Procedural Representation of Three-Dimensional Objects,* IBM Journal of Research and Development, 20, Nov. 1976, 582-589.

[30] Hanson, A., and E. Riseman; *The Design of a Semantically Directed Vision Processor,* Computer and Information Science Dept. Tech. Report 75C-1, Univ. of Massachusetts, Feb. 1975.

[31] Hollerbach, John; *Hierarchical Shape Description of Objects by Selection and Modification of Prototypes,* MIT AI-TR-346, Nov. 1975.

[32] Horn, B.K.P.; *Obtaining Shape from Shading Information,* in *The Psychology of Computer Vision,* P.H. Winston ed., McGraw-Hill, 1975.

[33] Kanade, Takeo; *Model Representations and Control Structures in Image Understanding,* Proc. of IJCAI-5, Cambridge, Aug. 1977, 1074-1082.

[34] de Kleer, Johan, and Gerald Jay Sussman; *Propagation of Constraints Applied to Circuit Synthesis,* MIT AIM-485, Sep. 1978.

[35] Lieberman, L.; *Model-Driven Vision for Industrial Automation,* in *Advances in Digital Image Processing: Theory, Application, Implementation,* Peter Stucki, ed., Plenum Press, 1979.

[36] Lowe, David; *Solving for the Parameters of Object Models from Image Descriptions,* Proceedings ARPA Image Understanding Workshop, College Park, MD, April 1980, 121-127.

[37] Lozano-Pérez, Tomás; *The Design of a Mechanical Assembly System,* MIT AI-TR-397, Dec. 1976.

[38] Lozano-Pérez, Tomás, and Michael A. Wesley; *An Algorithm for Planning Collision-Free Paths Among Polyhedral Obstacles,* CACM 22, Oct. 1979, 560-570.

[39] Marr, David; *Visual Information Processing: The structure and creation of visual representations,* Proceedings IJCAI-6, Tokyo, August 1979, 1108-1126.

[40] Marr, David, and Ellen Hildreth; *Theory of Edge Detection,* MIT AIM-518, April 1979.

[41] Marr, D., and H.K. Nishihara; *Representation and Recognition of the Spatial Organization of Three Dimensional Shapes,* MIT AIM-377, Aug. 1976.

[42] McDermott, Drew; *A Theory of Metric Spatial Inference,* Proceedings of the First Annual National Conference of on Artificial Intelligence, sponsored by the AAAI, Stanford, Aug. 1980, 246-248.

[43] Michie, Donald; *Memo Functions: A Language Feature with Rote-Learning Properties,* Proceedings IFIP 1968.

[44] Miyamoto, Eiichi, and Thomas O. Binford; *Display Generated by a Generalized Cone Representation,* IEEE Conference on Computer Graphics and Image Processing, May 1975.

[45] Moravec, Hans Peter; *Obstacle Avoidance and Navigation in the Real World by a Seeing Robot Rover,* Stanford AI Lab Memo AIM-340, Sept. 1980.

[46] Nevatia, Ramakant, and K. Ramesh Babu; *Linear Feature Extraction and Description,* Computer Graphics and Image Processing 13, 1980, 257-269.

[47] Nevatia, Ramakant, and Thomas O. Binford; *Description and Recognition of Curved Objects,* Artificial Intelligence 8(1977), 77-98.

[48] Ohta, Yu-ichi, Takeo Kanade, and Toshiyuki Sakai; *A Production System for Region Analysis,* Proceedings IJCAI-6, Tokyo, August 1979, 684-686.

[49] Requicha, Aristides A.G.; *Representations for Rigid Solids: Theory, Methods, and Systems,* Computing Surveys, Vol 12, No. 4, Dec. 1980, 437-464.

[50] Rubin, Steven M.; *The ARGOS Image Understanding System,* Proceedings ARPA Image Understanding Workshop, Pittsburgh, PA, Nov. 1978, 159-162.

[51] Salisbury, J. Kenneth; *Active Stiffness Control of a Manipulator in Cartesian Coordinates,* 19th IEEE Conference on Decision and Control, Albuquerque, NM, Dec. 1980.

[52] Shapiro, Linda G., John D. Moriarty, Prasanna G. Mulgaonkar, and Robert M. Haralick; *Sticks, Plates, and Blobs: A Three-Dimensional Object Representation for Scene Analysis,* Proceedings of the First Annual National Conference on Artificial Intelligence, sponsored by the AAAI, Stanford, Aug. 1980, 28-30.

[53] Shostak, Robert E.; *On the SUP—INF Method for Proving Presburger Formulas,* JACM 24, 1977, 529-543.

[54] Soroka, Barry I.; *Understanding Objects from Slices: Extracting Generalized Cylinder Descriptions from Serial Sections,* TR-79-1, Dept. of Computer Science, University of Kansas, 1979.

[55] Soroka, Barry I.; *Debugging Manipulator Programs with a Simulator,* Autofact West Conference, Society of Manufacturing Engineers, Anaheim, Nov. 1980.

[56] Stallman, Richard, and Gerald Jay Sussman; *Forward Reasoning and Dependency-Directed Backtracking in a System for Computer-Aided Circuit Analysis,* Artificial Intelligence 9, 1977, 135-196.

[57] Sugihara, Kokichi; *Automatic Construction of Junction Dictionaries and their Exploitation for the Analysis of Range Data,* Proceedings of IJCAI-79, Tokyo, Aug. 1979, 859-864.

[58] Taylor, Russell Highsmith; *A Synthesis of Manipulator Control Programs From Task-Level Specifications,* Stanford AI Lab Memo, AIM-282, July 1976.

[59] Voelcker, H.B., A.A.G. Requicha, E.E. Hartquist, W.B. Fisher, J.E. Shapiro, and N.K. Birrell; *An Introduction to PADL: Characteristics, Status, and Rationale,* Production Automation Project Technical Memorandum TM-22, University of Rochester, Dec. 1974.

[60] Waltz, David; *Understanding Line Drawings of Scenes with Shadows,* in *The Psychology of Computer Vision,* P.H. Winston ed., McGraw-Hill, 1975.

[61] Winston, Patrick H.; *Learning Structural Descriptions from Examples,* in *The Psychology of Computer Vision,* P.H. Winston ed., McGraw-Hill, 1975.

[62] Woodham, Robert J.; *Relating Properties of Surface Curvature to Image Intensity,* Proceedings of IJCAI-79, Tokyo, Aug. 1979, 971-977.

Index